The Diagnostic Manual of Herpesvirus Infections

Thomas P. Habif

Adjunct Associate Professor of
Medicine (Dermatology)
Dartmouth Medical School
Hanover, New Hampshire

Acknowledgement

Grateful appreciation is extended
to James J. Vredenburgh, MD,
for his contribution to this publication.

Burroughs Wellcome Co.
3030 Cornwallis Road
Research Triangle Park, NC 27709

Published in association with Clinical Communications Inc.
Greenwich, Connecticut

ISBN: 1-57013-005-1

ZC-Y04115
Printed in the United States of America

Introduction

This book is intended to help promote an understanding of a complicated subject. Every individual becomes infected with one or several members of the herpes family of viruses at some time during his or her life. The virus then is incorporated into the genetic material and resides there permanently; it is always lurking undercover. This association is usually of limited consequence as long as we remain healthy, with strong immunity. All of the herpesviruses except varicella zoster periodically become reactivated and shed virus particles that may be infectious to others, but do not cause disease in the immunocompetent host. However, if one's immunity becomes depressed, the virus seizes the opportunity and turns on its host. Sun exposure, upper respiratory infections, or fevers allow the herpes simplex virus to emerge and attack. HIV infection or immunocompromise following chemotherapy or during organ transplantation makes a person vulnerable to any of the herpesviruses. They then have the potential for widespread infection and can be fatal.

Primary or first-episode infection with any member of the herpesvirus family is best tolerated when it occurs during preadolescence. These infections can be asymptomatic. Symptomatic reactivation of two members of this family, herpes simplex and herpes zoster, can occur in immunocompetent individuals. They both cause a vesicular eruption, pain, and lymphadenopathy, and heal without treatment. There are two aspects that make these diseases important. Herpes simplex infections can recur symptomatically for years, and herpes zoster can recur once and cause sustained, disabling pain.

Contents

The Family *Herpesviridae*

There are almost 80 herpesviruses that infect many different animals. Six known members of the family *Herpesviridae* infect humans: herpes simplex virus types 1 and 2, varicella-zoster virus, cytomegalovirus, Epstein-Barr virus, and human herpesvirus type 6.

Herpesviruses are ubiquitous, and most humans become infected. The herpesviruses have a similar architecture, induce lifelong latent infection after the primary infection, and reactivate at intervals.[1] For any herpesvirus, latency occurs within small numbers of very specific types of cells.

Herpesviruses vary in their abilities to infect different cell types. Herpes simplex and varicella-zoster viruses grow in human epithelial cells; Epstein-Barr virus can only be cultivated in B lymphocytes. Herpesviruses are fragile and do not survive in the environment. They are usually acquired by intimate contact with infected body fluid. Many infections are transmitted from an asymptomatic person. The episodes of asymptomatic shedding probably exceed those of symptomatic shedding.

All herpesviruses are large (150 to 250 nm), DNA-containing, enveloped viruses that are composed of four elements (Figs 1-3).[1] The outer envelope contains glycoprotein spikes; a capsid surrounds the core; and an amorphous material called the tegument fills the space between the capsid and the envelope. The internal core consists of proteins and the viral genome (linear double-stranded DNA).

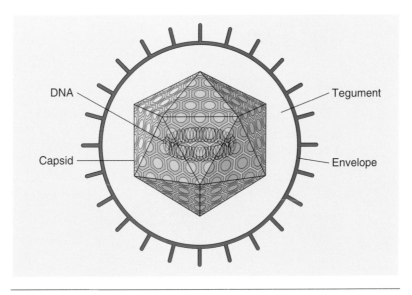

Fig 1.—Morphology of a herpesvirus.

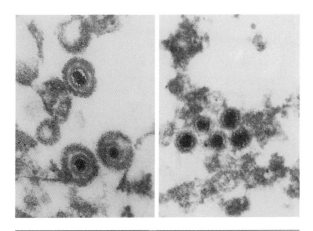

Fig 2.—Herpes simplex virus. Electron micrograph showing the characteristic enveloped virions. (Courtesy of Boris Gueft, MD)

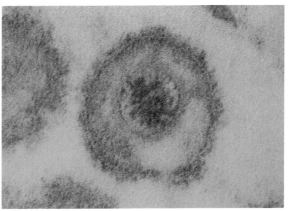

Fig 3.—Structure of the herpes simplex virus. Electron micrograph showing a complete enveloped virion. (Courtesy of Boris Gueft, MD)

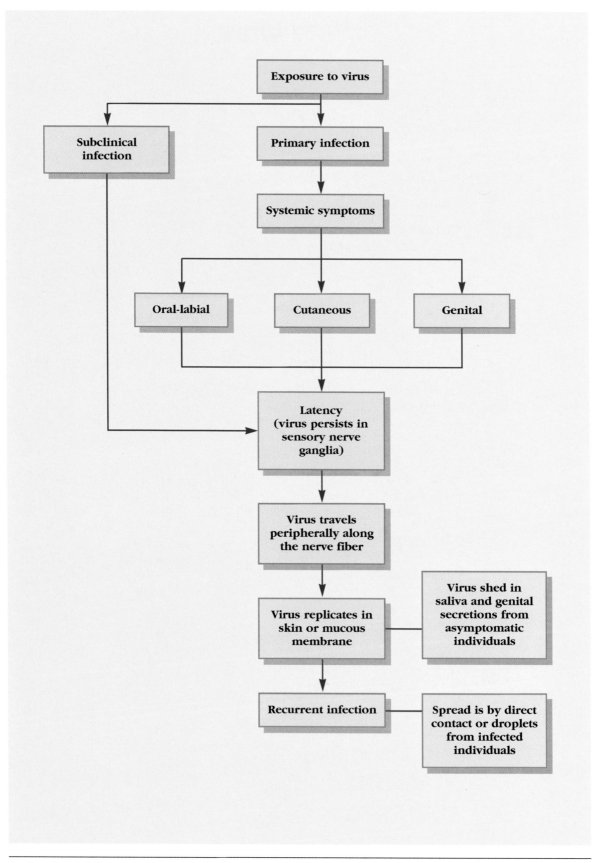

Fig 4.—The clinical course of herpes simplex virus types 1 and 2 infections.

Herpes Simplex Virus Infection

Two virus types cause herpes simplex virus (HSV) infections: HSV-1 and HSV-2. Both types produce identical infection patterns. HSV infections have primary and secondary (recurrent) phases (Fig 4). During the primary phase (Fig 5) the virus enters the nerve endings in the skin directly below the lesions (Fig 6) and ascends through peripheral nerves to the dorsal root ganglia where it remains in a latent stage. The secondary phase (Fig 7) is characterized by recurrent disease at the same site. Infections can occur anywhere on the skin or mucous membranes. Infection in one area does not protect the patient from subsequent infection at a different site. Lesions are intraepidermal and usually heal without scarring.

Infection in the immunocompromised patient

Immunocompromised patients who have defects in cell-mediated immunity have more severe and extensive infections than do those who have deficits in humoral immunity. These infections are an important cause of morbidity and mortality in patients with human immunodeficiency virus (HIV) infection or hematologic malignancies (such as Hodgkin's disease), in bone marrow transplant recipients, in organ transplant recipients (predominantly from the necessary immunosuppressant medications), in burn or trauma patients on mechanical ventilation, and in patients receiving steroids, cyclophosphamide, azathioprine, or other immunosuppressants for other conditions. The spectrum of disease varies widely. Immunocompromised patients may have self-limited disease; however, they typically experience infections that are severe, extensive, and prolonged, and that recur more frequently. Herpes simplex virus infections of the esophagus, liver, and lung occur in immunocompromised patients. Infections of these organs are almost never seen in immunocompetent persons.

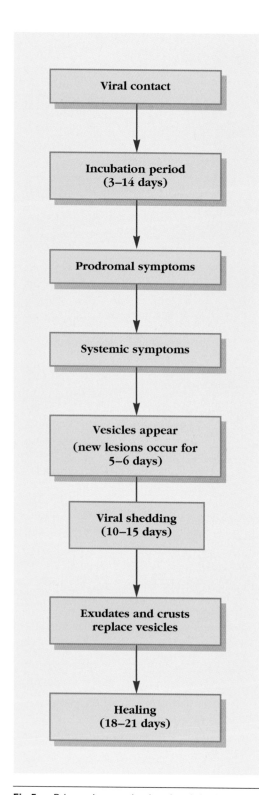

Viral contact

↓

**Incubation period
(3–14 days)**

↓

Prodromal symptoms

↓

Systemic symptoms

↓

**Vesicles appear
(new lesions occur for
5–6 days)**

↓

**Viral shedding
(10–15 days)**

↓

**Exudates and crusts
replace vesicles**

↓

**Healing
(18–21 days)**

Fig 5.—Primary herpes simplex virus infection. A primary infection is characterized by many vesicles, systemic symptoms, and painful, tender regional lymphadenopathy.

Primary infection

Transmission

The virus is spread by respiratory droplets, by direct contact with an active lesion, or by virus-containing fluid such as saliva or cervical secretions.

Incubation

Symptoms occur 3 to 14 or more days after contact.

Prodrome

Tenderness, pain, mild paresthesias, or burning occur at the site of inoculation. Some patients have no symptoms.

Symptoms

Tender lymphadenopathy, headache, generalized aching, and fever occur. Disease severity increases with age. Many infections are asymptomatic and a rise in antibody titer will be the only evidence of disease.

Lesions

Grouped vesicles on an erythematous base appear, become depressed in the center (umbilicated), erode, and then crust (Fig 6). Vesicles are numerous and scattered (more so than in the recurrent phase) and are uniform in size (in contrast to the vesicles seen in herpes zoster that vary in size). Lesions in the mouth, vagina, and under the foreskin accumulate exudate, whereas skin lesions form a crust.

In the immunocompromised patient, the primary infection is generally more severe with increased tissue destruction. The typical grouped vesicles frequently are not seen, but rather erosions, ulcerations, denuded areas, or eschar are likely to be present. The primary infection can occur anywhere, but the mouth, lips, penis, vulva, vagina, or perianal areas are the most common sites. Importantly, the frequency of disseminated primary HSV infection with pneumonitis, hepatitis, and/or encephalitis is much higher than in immunocompetent patients.

Duration

Lesions last 2 to 3 weeks unless secondarily infected.

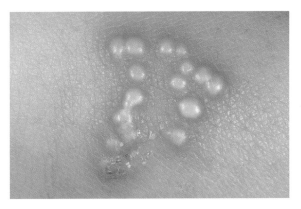

A. Vesicles of a uniform size appear on a red base.

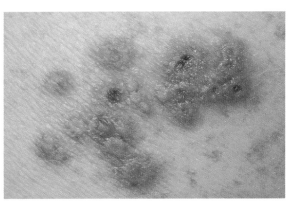

B. The centers become depressed (umbilicated).

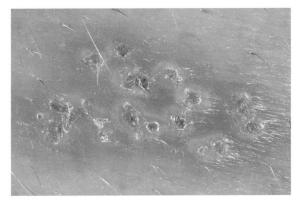

C. Crusts replace vesicles.

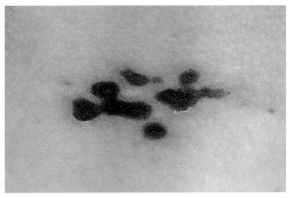

D. Crusting of the entire base is followed by healing with or without scarring.

Fig 6.—The evolution of herpes simplex virus lesions.

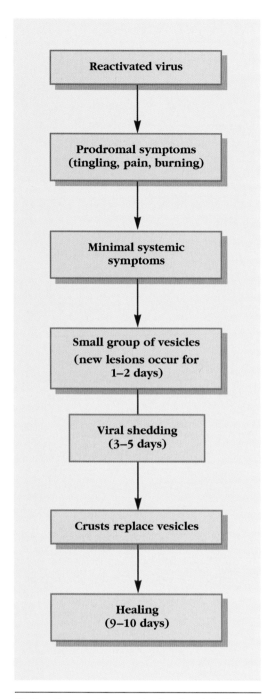

Fig 7.—Recurrent herpes simplex virus infection. In contrast to a primary infection, a recurrent infection is characterized by a limited number of vesicles, few systemic symptoms, and usually no lymphadenopathy.

Recurrent infection

Risk factors
In persons with normal immune systems, factors such as stress, sexual activity, local skin trauma, ultraviolet (UV) light exposure, menses, fatigue, or fever can reactivate the virus, which then travels down the peripheral nerves to the site of initial infection.

Prodrome
Symptoms last 2 to 24 hours and resemble those of the primary infection.

Symptoms
Lymphadenopathy and systemic symptoms are usually not present or are less intense than during the primary infection.

Lesions
Dome-shaped, tense vesicles rapidly form on an erythematous base and umbilicate. New lesions occur for 1 to 2 days. In 2 to 4 days they rupture, forming either aphthae-like erosions in the mouth, vaginal area, or under the foreskin, or erosions covered by crusts on the lips and skin. Viral shedding occurs for 3 to 5 days. Crusts are shed in about 8 days.

In the immunocompromised patient, recurrent infection is more severe, frequently with a fulminant course with marked tissue destruction and early dissemination. The lesions may be papules, vesicles, erosions, ulcers, or excoriations. Because of the tissue destruction, the lesions heal slowly and residual scarring is common.

Frequency
Recurrent infection is not inevitable; the recurrence rate is unpredictable. Many people experience a decrease in the frequency of recurrence with time, while others experience an increase. The frequency of recurrence varies with anatomic site and virus type.[1] HSV-2 genital infections recur six times more frequently than HSV-1 genital infections. The frequency of recurrence of HSV-2 genital herpes is higher than that of HSV-1 oral-labial infection. HSV-1 oral infections recur more often than genital HSV-1 infections. The frequency of recurrence is lowest for oral-labial HSV-2 infections. Many individuals never experience recurrence.[1]

Laboratory diagnosis

The clinical presentation is usually so characteristic that an accurate diagnosis can be made by inspection. The sensitivity of all laboratory methods depends on the stage of lesions (sensitivity is higher in vesicular than in ulcerative lesions); on whether the patient has a primary or a recurrent episode of the disease (sensitivity is higher in first episodes); and on whether the sample is from an immunocompromised or an immunocompetent patient (more antigen is found in immunocompromised patients).

A number of laboratory procedures are available if confirmation is desired.[2]

Culture

The most definitive method for diagnosis is culture. Viral culture is the most efficient means of confirming the clinical diagnosis in women with a first-episode infection. The virus can appear at several different sites in the genitourinary tract. Obtaining a sample from a single site has a sensitivity of about 60% in confirming the diagnosis. The insertion of separate swabs from a number of anatomical sites into one culture vial is the most efficient and cost-effective way to collect genital samples for viral culture.

Collection

It is best to sample lesions in the vesicular or early ulcerative stage. Resolving lesions (usually 5 days or more) are not generally productive. Vesicles are punctured and a swab is then rubbed onto the base of the lesion. Cervical samples are taken from the endocervix or erosions, if present, with a swab.

Interpretation

Presence of viral antigens or cytopathic changes is demonstrable within 24 hours, and more than 90% of virus-containing specimens become positive after 3 days. Cultures are monitored for characteristic morphologic changes and cytopathic effects for up to 5 to 7 days after inoculation for maximum sensitivity.

Serology

Because of the high incidence of antibodies to herpes simplex in the population, assay of a single serum specimen is not of great value. The test does not discriminate between antibodies to HSV-1 and those to HSV-2. IgG and IgM are measured in separate tests. Normal titers are less than 1:5 for both IgG and IgM.

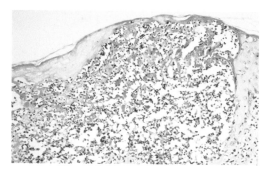

A. An intraepidermal vesicle, the primary lesion.

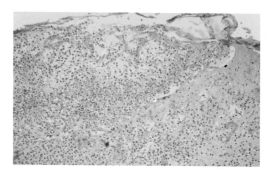

B. There is a sparse to moderate lymphohistiocytic infiltrate around the dilated blood vessels in the dermis.

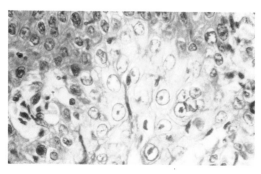

C. Epithelial cells. There is abundant pale staining cytoplasm. The nuclei contain dense eosinophilic central inclusions surrounded by a clear halo (Cowdry type A inclusion body).

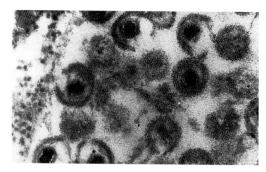

D. This electron micrograph shows viral bodies within intranuclear inclusions. (Courtesy of Boris Gueft, MD)

Fig 8.—Herpes simplex histology.

The presence of IgM or a fourfold or greater rise in IgG titer indicates recent infection. The convalescent sample should be drawn 2 to 3 weeks after the acute specimen is drawn. The presence of IgG indicates past exposure and immunity.

Subtyping

There are two serotypes of HSV. HSV-l infections are primarily oropharyngeal; HSV-2 infections are primarily genital. Subtyping can be helpful for epidemiologic study and patient counseling, but is not commonly done in office practice.

Polymerase chain reaction

Polymerase chain reaction is a recently developed technique that permits the isolation and rapid duplication of specific deoxyribonucleic acid (DNA) fragments. This technique is most useful for specimens that are complex (such as tissue homogenates), impure, or present in minute amounts. The DNA may be either fragmented or intact.

The three-stage chemical laboratory procedure is performed in a single test tube over a 4- to 6-hour period. It is highly sensitive and specific. Minute fragments of DNA are propagated (amplified) more than a million-fold during this short period of time and then analyzed by electrophoresis. Tiny specimens such as formalin-fixed paraffin-embedded skin biopsies can be extracted with xylene and identified. This technique was used to detect HSV-specific DNA in the biopsy tissue of patients with erythema multiforme.[3]

Histopathology

Diagnosis of cutaneous herpes infection rarely requires biopsy; but, if indicated, an intact vesicle should be sampled. The histologic picture is characteristic but not unique for herpes simplex (Fig 8). The lesion is an intraepidermal vesicle that contains infected, degenerated epithelial cells.

The epithelial spinous cells become "ballooned" with abundant, pale-staining eosinophilic cytoplasm. Ballooned cells lose their intracellular bridges and separate from surrounding cells. Some of the distended, ballooned cells rupture their membranes and coalesce with adjacent cells to form multinucleated giant cells.

Nuclear changes are seen in infected cells of the skin and other organs. The nucleus becomes enlarged with homogenization of the nuclear contents, referred to as a "ground-glass" appearance. The homogeneous material condenses, shrinks away from the nuclear membrane and becomes localized in the center of the nucleus. The centrally located eosinophilic mass is surrounded by a clear halo and is termed a Cowdry type A inclusion body.

Tzanck smear

Collection

Best results are obtained from intact vesicles. Remove the vesicle roof and scrape the underlying moist skin with a #15 surgical blade (vesicular fluid is not to be used). Smear the material onto a glass slide.

Staining methods

Method 1: Fix the material for 1 minute with absolute alcohol, and then stain with Giemsa or Wright's stain.

Method 2: Add toluidine blue 0.1% aqueous solution to an air-dried slide specimen and rinse off with tap water in 15 seconds. Air drying is repeated, and a cover glass is applied over a permanent mounting medium.

Method 3: A fast method using a commercially available series of solutions (Diffquik®) is used in many laboratories. The material can be stained in approximately 1 minute.

Interpretation

Giant cells with 2 to 15 nuclei are the characteristic finding (Fig 9). Recently infected cells contain a single enlarged nucleus with a thick membrane. Later, the cells begin to fuse and become multinucleated, and the nuclear membrane continues to thicken. Characteristic granular, eosinophilic, intranuclear inclusions then appear (seen only with the Papanicolaou stain).

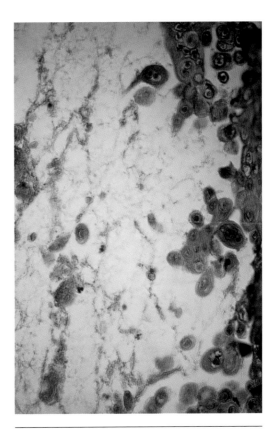

Fig 9.—Tzanck smear. Multinucleated giant cells with thickened nuclear membranes.

Papanicolaou smear

This technique is useful for detecting HSV-infected cells in cervical tissue from women without symptoms; routine smears often reveal unsuspected herpesvirus infection.

Collection

The cells are smeared onto a slide, fixed with 95% ethanol or commercial fixative, stained with Papanicolaou stain, and observed under the microscope.

Interpretation

Recently infected cells contain a single enlarged nucleus with a thick membrane. Later, the cells begin to fuse and become multinucleated, and the nuclear membrane continues to thicken. Characteristic granular, eosinophilic, intranuclear inclusions then appear.

Rapid methods

A diagnosis can be made within a few hours by visualization of HSV antigens in cells of smears from secretions using rapid immunofluorescent or ELISA-based diagnostic methods.

Oral-Labial Herpes Simplex

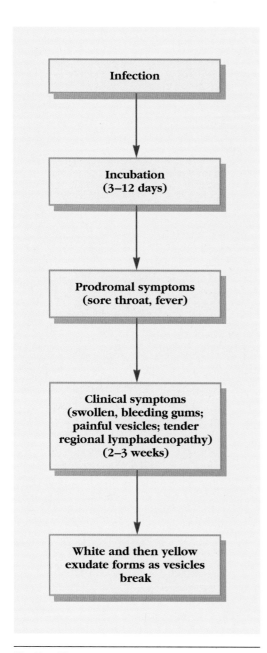

Fig 10.—The course of herpetic gingivostomatitis, a frequent manifestation of HSV-1.

Oral-labial infection (eg, gingivostomatitis and pharyngitis) is a frequent manifestation of first-episode HSV-1 infection. HSV-2 occurs in this area, but less frequently. Infection occurs most commonly in children aged 1 to 5 years, and usually lasts 2 to 3 weeks (Fig 10).

Primary infection

Incubation
The incubation period is 3 to 12 days.

Prodrome
Sore throat and fever may precede the onset of vesicles.

Symptoms
Most cases are mild; some are severe. Pain interferes with eating, and tender cervical lymphadenopathy develops.

Lesions
Painful vesicles can occur anywhere in the oral cavity, and may be extensive over the lips and lower face (Fig 11). The oral vesicles rapidly coalesce and erode with a white and then yellow, superficial, purulent exudate.

In the immunocompromised patient, lesions generally are associated with more tissue destruction and, less commonly, vesicle formation. Deep ulceration or excoriation may occur, and lesions are more extensive both in size and number. Up to 20% of allogenic bone marrow transplant patients who are seronegative will develop a primary HSV infection.

Course
Fever subsides 3 to 5 days after onset, and oral pain and erosions are usually gone in 2 weeks; in severe cases, these symptoms may last for 3 weeks. Herpes infections are severe and extensive in immunocompromised patients.

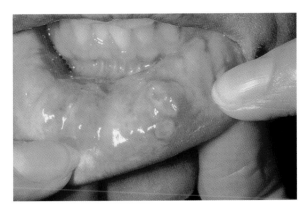

A. Painful vesicles occur in the oral cavity.

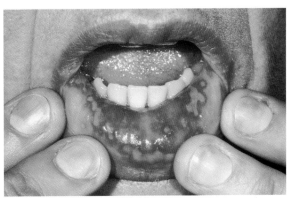

B. The vesicles rapidly coalesce and erode, leaving a white and then yellow, superficial, purulent exudate.

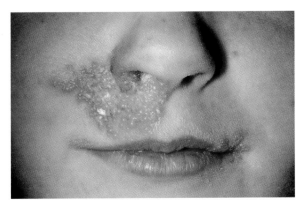

C. Intense vesiculation at two sites. The intense vesiculation covers a much wider area than in most recurrent infections, and the vesicles extend into the nasal passage.

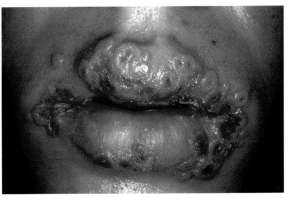

D. Extensive vesiculation over upper and lower lips. Unusually large vesicles show prominent umbilication.

Fig 11.—Primary oral-labial herpes simplex infection may be severe with extensive lesions at multiple sites including the lips, lower face, and nasal passages.

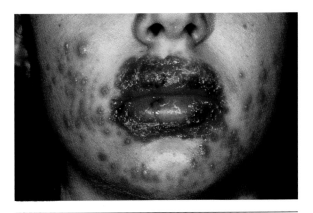

Fig 12.—Primary oral-labial herpes simplex infection in an immunocompromised patient, a young girl who was taking prednisone.

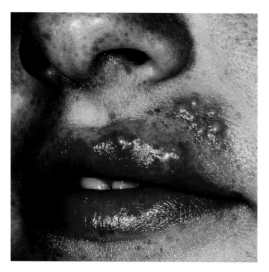

A. Sunlight was a factor in initiating this painful recurrence at two sites on the upper lip.

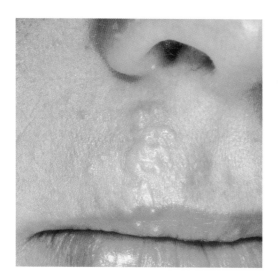

B. Only moderate discomfort was associated with these small vesicles on a noninflamed base.

Fig 13.—Recurrent herpes simplex labialis.

Recurrent infection

Risk factors

Fever (fever blisters), upper respiratory infections (cold sores), and exposure to UV light may reactivate the virus and precede the onset of a recurrence.

Lesions

The most common manifestation is eruptions on the vermillion border of the lip—recurrent herpes simplex labialis (Fig 13); recurrent lesions can appear as a localized cluster of small ulcers in the oral cavity.

In the immunocompromised patient, recurrent HSV infection is more severe, with less predilection for certain sites. There is significantly more tissue destruction and less inflammation and vesicle formation (Fig 14). The lesions progress and disseminate rapidly.

Recurrent infections are common following immunosuppressive therapy, particularly myeloablative therapy with bone marrow transplantation or organ transplantation. Up to 60% of allogenic bone marrow transplant recipients who are seropositive will develop recurrent infection.

Frequency

Recurrences average 2 to 3 each year, but may happen as often as 12 times a year. Oral HSV-1 infections recur more often than oral HSV-2 infections.

Prevention

Opaque creams such as zinc oxide or sun-blocking agents incorporated into a lip balm will discourage, but not completely prevent, infection.

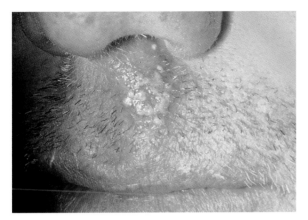

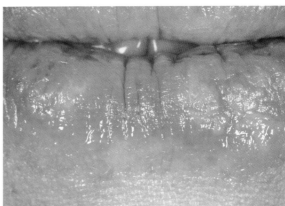

C. Recurrence on the upper lip or in the nasal passage without involvement of the vermillion border is common.

D. Painful swelling and vesiculation of the entire lower lip followed sun exposure.

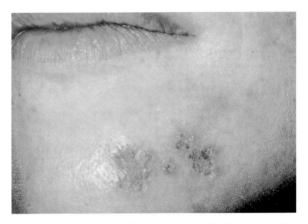

E. The diagnosis of herpes simplex is suspected in the absence of vesicles. Grouped uniform erosions are characteristic.

Fig 13.—*(Cont'd)*

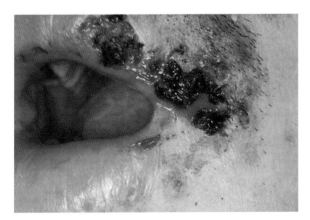

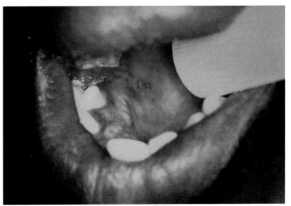

A. Atresia of the lip in a 47-year-old man with rheumatoid arthritis requiring immunosuppressant therapy.

B. Severe infection in a patient undergoing induction chemotherapy for acute leukemia.

Fig 14.—Recurrent herpes simplex labialis in immunocompromised patients.

Cutaneous Herpes Simplex

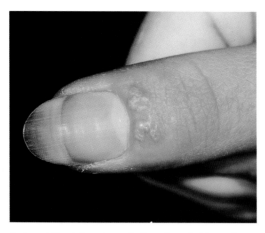

A. Inoculation followed examination of a patient's mouth.

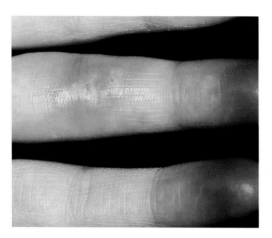

B. Autoinoculation in an adult woman with a genital herpetic lesion.

Fig 15.—Cutaneous herpes simplex. Infection of the finger (herpetic whitlow).

Herpes simplex may appear on any skin surface or mucosal membrane. It is important to identify all the characteristic features when attempting to differentiate cutaneous herpes from other vesicular eruptions. Herpes simplex of the finger (herpetic whitlow) can resemble a group of warts or a bacterial infection (Fig 15).

Herpetic whitlow

Herpes simplex of the finger is most often seen in children with gingivostomatitis and in women with genital herpes. (Health-care professionals who had contact with oral secretions used to be the most commonly affected group; the incidence has decreased as a result of stricter infection control precautions.)

Buttock infection

Herpes simplex of the buttock area is much more common in women (Fig 16). The reason for this is not known.

Eruptions in immunocompromised patients

In immunocompromised patients, cutaneous or mucosal HSV infection is generally more severe with more tissue destruction (Fig 17). Lesions are more erosive or ulcerative and extensive. Cutaneous or mucosal herpetic infection is more common in areas of tissue destruction, such as cutaneous tumor involvement or areas of severe mucositis from chemotherapy or radiotherapy. It is frequently difficult to detect herpetic infections in these areas, so a high index of suspicion is required. Lesions may take significantly longer to heal and residual scarring is common.

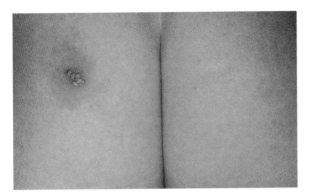

A. The early vesicular stage.

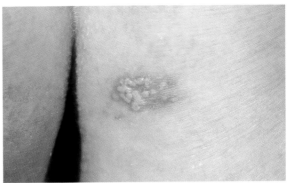

B. The vesicles are beginning to coalesce in this painful recurrent lesion. Recurrence may not be in exactly the same location.

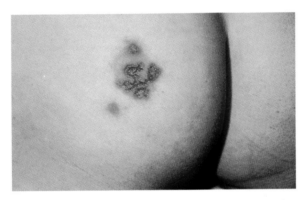

C. The diagnosis of herpes simplex is suspected in the absence of vesicles. Grouped uniform erosions are characteristic. This lesion healed with scarring after some of the erosions extended into the dermis to form ulcers.

Fig 16.—Cutaneous herpes simplex. Buttock infection.

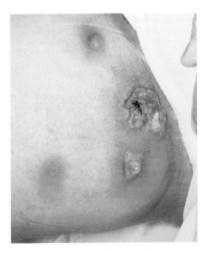

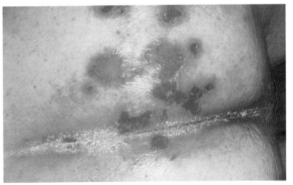

B. Severe perirectal infection in 63-year-old patient with chronic lymphocytic leukemia requiring chemotherapy and steroids.

A. Severe infection in 23-year-old man 8 months after a heart transplant.

Fig 17.—Cutaneous herpes simplex. Buttock infections in immunocompromised patients.

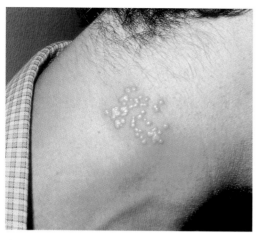

A. This lesion appeared 6 days after a wrestling match.

Herpes gladiatorum

Trauma facilitates transfer of the herpes virus, especially to fully keratinized skin. The herpes virus may be transmitted by wrestling contact (Fig 18).

Trunk infection and other areas

Herpes simplex of the lumbosacral region or trunk may be very difficult to differentiate from herpes zoster, with the diagnosis becoming apparent only at the time of recurrence (Fig 19). Lesions of herpes zoster do not typically form on the midline.

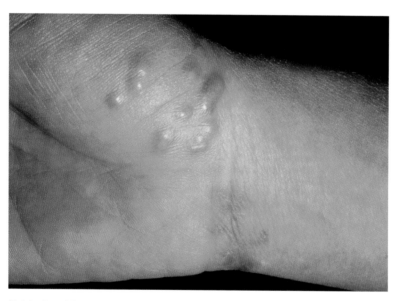

B. Infection of the palm occurred several days following a wrestling match. The vesicles are large on the thick skin of the palm.

Fig 18.—Cutaneous herpes simplex. Herpes gladiatorum.

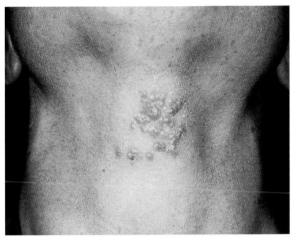

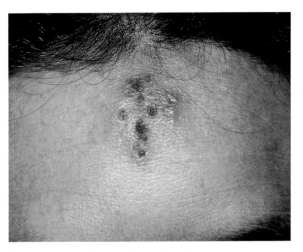

A. A single group of vesicles of uniform size is characteristic of herpes simplex. (Lesions of herpes zoster do not typically form on the midline and the vesicles of herpes zoster vary in size.)

B. Lesions have evolved into the crusting stage.

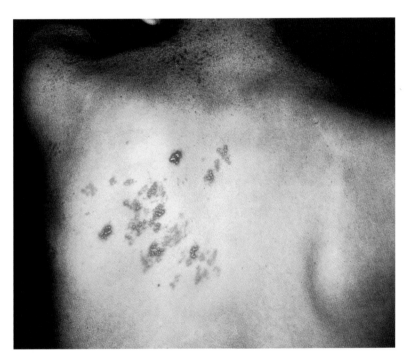

C. Herpes simplex of the lumbosacral region or trunk may be difficult to differentiate from herpes zoster or poison ivy. Cultures and antibody titers help make the diagnosis.

Fig 19.—Cutaneous herpes simplex.

Eczema Herpeticum

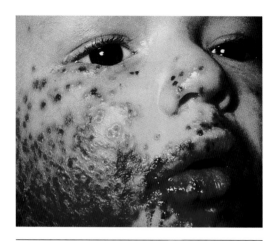

Fig 20.—Eczema herpeticum. This extensive eruption occurred following contact with a parent who had herpes labialis. The child is atopic but did not have dermatitis at the time.

Eczema herpeticum (Figs 20-22) is the association of two common conditions: atopic dermatitis and herpes simplex virus infection.[4] Certain atopic infants and adults may develop the rapid onset of diffuse cutaneous herpes simplex, ranging from mild and transient to fatal.[4,5] The disease is most common in areas of active or recently healed atopic dermatitis, particularly the face, but normal skin can be involved. Most cases of eczema herpeticum occur in the second and third decades.

Source of infection

A history of herpes labialis in a parent occurring in the previous week is obtained in one third of all cases.

Primary infection

The disease in most cases is a primary herpes simplex infection.

Recurrent infection

Recurrences are uncommon and usually limited. Recurrent disease is milder and typically without constitutional symptoms.

Course

With primary infection, about 10 days after exposure, numerous vesicles develop, become pustular, and umbilicate markedly. New crops of vesicles may appear during the following weeks. The most intense viral dissemination is located in the areas of dermatitis, but normal-appearing skin may be involved.

Systemic symptoms

High fever and adenopathy occur 2 to 3 days after the onset of vesiculation. The fever subsides in 4 to 5 days in uncomplicated cases, and the lesions evolve in the typical manner.

Complications

Secondary staphylococcal infection commonly occurs. Viremia with infection of internal organs can be fatal.

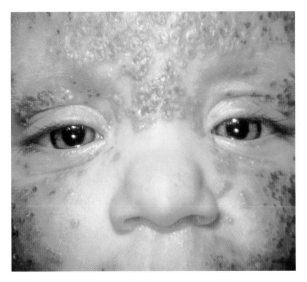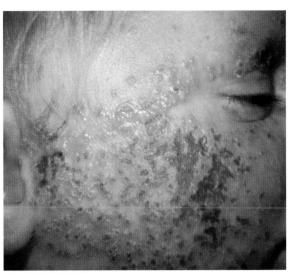

A. Numerous umbilicated vesicles have become confluent on the forehead and cheeks.

B. New lesions are forming as the first crop enters the crusting stage.

Fig 21.—Eczema herpeticum.

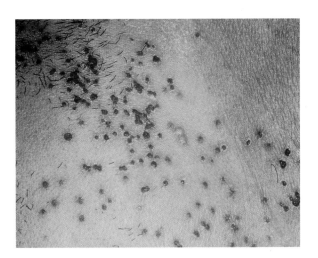

Fig 22.—Eczema herpeticum in a 26-year-old man with active atopic dermatitis who had recurrent herpes labialis 1 week prior to this extensive eruption; the first crop of lesions have formed crusts; the two vesicles in the center herald the onset of a new crop of lesions.

Infection of Burns

Herpesvirus infections are commonly seen in immuno-compromised patients and may account for considerable morbidity and some mortality. In one study, 52% of patients with severe burn injuries became infected with either HSV or cytomegalovirus (CMV) or both.[6] HSV infection was associated with older age, tracheal intubation, facial burn, inhalation injury, length of hospitalization, and the presence of full-thickness burn (Fig 23). The risk of CMV infection increases with the duration of hospitalization and with the depth of the burn. Transfusion of blood products was not correlated with an increased incidence of primary or reactivation of CMV infections. There was no significant association of HSV or CMV with mortality.[6]

Radiation therapy can produce significant tissue injury and burns; infection with HSV or CMV may occur in these areas. Similarly, chemotherapy can produce mucositis or esophagitis, with an increased risk of HSV or, less commonly, CMV infection. If an area of mucositis is slow to heal, new areas can develop significantly after the chemotherapy-induced mucositis appeared. Alternatively, a worsening clinical course—with increased symptoms following initial improvement, and then herpetic infection—may be the underlying etiology.

A. A patient with second- and third-degree burns with confluent herpetic ulcers involving the burned areas of the thigh and lower leg. (Courtesy of Frederick G. Hayden, MD. Reprinted with permission of The C.V. Mosby Company)

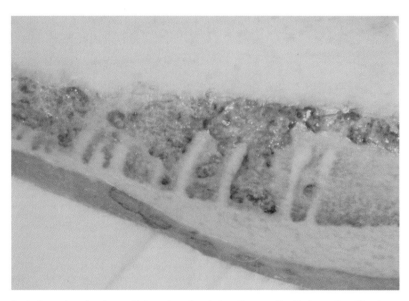

B. A closer view showing multiple and confluent ulcerations confined to burn sites. (Courtesy of Frederick G. Hayden, MD. Reprinted with permission of The C.V. Mosby Company)

Fig 23.—Herpes simplex infection in a burn patient.

Genital Herpes Simplex

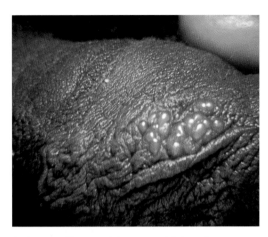

A. A group of tense vesicles appeared 5 days after sexual intercourse.

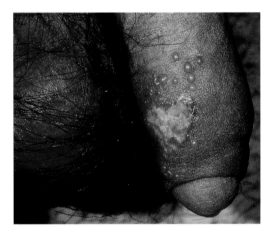

B. A group of vesicles have ruptured, leaving a broad erosion.

Fig 24.—Primary genital herpes simplex infection.

Herpes simplex infection of the penis, vulva, and rectum is pathophysiologically identical to herpes infection in other areas. Herpes genitalis (Figs 24-29) is primarily a disease of sexually active young adults. Both males and females who have no symptoms can transmit the disease. Infection can develop in males from contact with female carriers who have no obvious disease. The infection may be acquired from an active cervical infection or from cervical secretions of a female who chronically carries the virus. HSV-2 may not be an important etiologic factor in cervical cancer as was once suspected.

Psychosocial implications

Herpes has a tremendous psychosocial impact. The patient's response begins with initial shock and emotional numbing; a sense of loneliness and isolation follows. There are concerns about establishing relationships and that sexual gratification, marriage, and normal reproduction might not be possible. There is diminished self-esteem, social isolation, anxiety, and reluctance to initiate close relationships. Sexual drive persists, but there is a fear of initiating sexual relationships and an inhibition of sexual expression. A minority of patients experience deepening of depression with each recurrence, and all aspects of their lives are affected.

First-episode infections

Primary (never infected with HSV) and nonprimary (previous infection at another site) are the two types of first-episode infections.

Clinical course

First-episode infections are more extensive and have more systemic symptoms. Viral shedding lasts longer (15 to 16 days) in primary first-episode infections. The eruption frequently extends into the pubic area, and is possibly spread from secretions during sexual contact. The anal area may be involved by contamination with secretions and after anal intercourse.

Clinical characteristics

Bilaterally distributed, painful, multiple vesicles, pustules, or ulcers on the external genitalia, perineum, perianal area, or vaginal walls

or

Unilaterally distributed lesions accompanied by constitutional symptoms (with no history of such episodes)

Dysuria

and/or

Cervical necrosis

or

No symptoms

Complications

Simultaneous pharyngitis in 10% to 15% of patients, possibly from oral-genital contact.

Aspetic meningitis—fever, headache, and stiff neck—in 10% to 35% of patients.

Lab

Isolation of HSV from the genital tract

or

Serologic tests with antibody pattern that indicates no previous infection with HSV-2

Males

Extensive involvement, with edema and possible urinary retention, develops in males (Figs 24-27), especially if uncircumcised. Crusts do not form under the foreskin or in the anal area.

Females

Virus infections spread easily over moist surfaces. Females have more extensive disease and a higher incidence of constitutional symptoms because of the larger surface area involved (Fig 28). Wide areas of the female genitals may be covered with painful erosions. The cervix is involved in most cases, and erosive cervicitis is almost always associated with first-episode disease. Inflammation, edema, and pain may be so extreme that urination is interfered with and catheterization is required. The patient may be immobilized and require bed rest at home or in the hospital.

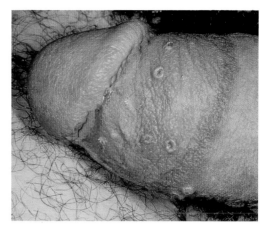

A. Vesicles may be discrete and scattered over a wide area. Recurrent disease manifests as a localized eruption.

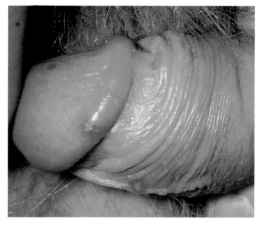

B. The crusts, like the vesicles, are not confluent. The diagnosis should be suspected even though primary lesions are absent.

Fig 25.—Primary genital herpes simplex.

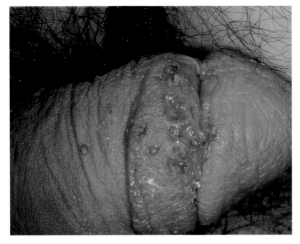

A. Vesicles under the foreskin rapidly become macerated and form erosions that may be filled with exudate.

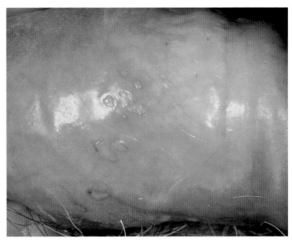

B. Crusts do not form in erosions that are located under the foreskin.

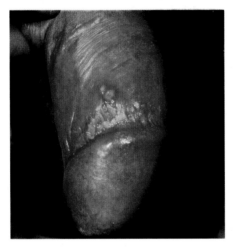

C. Erosions are concentrated on the prepuce.

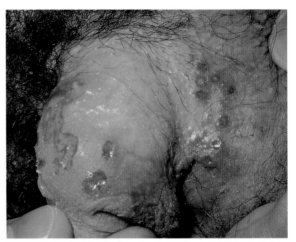

D. An extensive eruption on the shaft of the penis autoinoculated the scrotum. The erosions are deep and painful. (Chancroid has a similar appearance.)

Fig 26.—Primary genital herpes simplex.

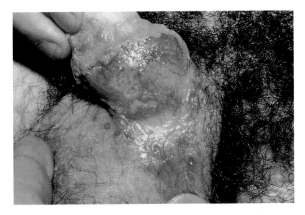

A. The erosions have become secondarily infected and confluent.

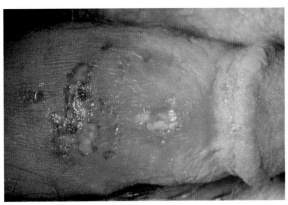

B. The shaft of the penis is red and painful as the erosions become confluent with a purulent base.

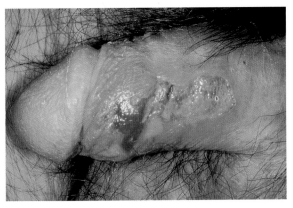

C. Erosions evolved into a large ulcer following a secondary Gram-negative bacterial infection.

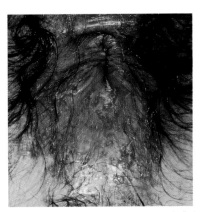

D. A massive inoculation of the anal area following anal intercourse.

Fig 27.—Primary genital herpes simplex. Secondary infection and extension of lesions.

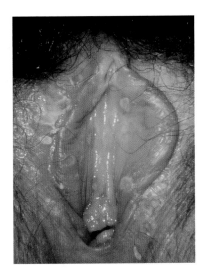

A. Vesicles become macerated and quickly form erosions on moist surfaces.

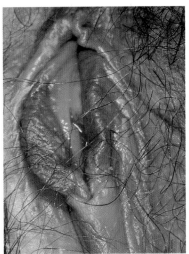

B. An acute painful eruption with erosions present on all surfaces of the vulva.

Fig 28.—Primary genital herpes simplex.

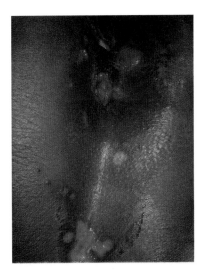

Fig 29.— Primary genital herpes simplex in a 73-year-old immunocompromised patient with Waldenström's macroglobulinemia.

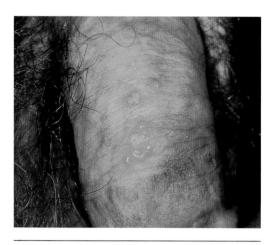

Fig 30.—Recurrent herpes simplex. A small group of vesicles and pustules have recurred on the same area for several months.

Recurrent infection

Clinical characteristics

Unilaterally distributed painful vesicles, pustules, or ulcers on the external genitalia (Fig 30), perineum, or perianal area

or

Bilateral small lesions and a history of similar episodes

or

Ulcers on the cervix without associated constitutional symptoms

Lab

Isolation of HSV from a genital lesion

or

The presence of HSV-2 antibodies

Females

Virus can only be isolated from the cervix in 10% to 15% of women with recurrent disease.

Rate

The recurrence rate varies with each individual and with the virus type.[1]

HSV-1

Recurrence is experienced in 50% of patients with primary HSV-1; the median time to first recurrence is 1 year.

HSV-2

HSV-2 genital infections occur six times more frequently than HSV-1 genital infections.[1] Recurrence is experienced in 95% of patients with primary HSV-2, with a median time to first recurrence of about 50 days. The median number of recurrences during the first year for patients with HSV-2 is four; 40% to 50% of patients have more than six recurrences per year. The recurrence rate stays at that level for at least 3 years.[7]

Risk factors for sexual transmission

Asymptomatic shedding

Asymptomatic or subclinical shedding of HSV is a major factor in the transmission of genital herpes infection. Even highly motivated couples who are aware of the signs and symptoms of genital herpes and attempt to avoid sexual contact with lesions remain at substantial risk for transmission of genital herpes to the uninfected partner. The risk of infection is greater for women. For heterosexual, white, monogamous couples in which one partner has a documented previous HSV infection, seronegative female susceptible partners have the highest risk for acquiring genital herpes infection. The risk is 17% for females and 4% for males. Previous HSV-1 infection reduces the risk for acquisition of HSV-2.

Males

The site of asymptomatic shedding in men is unknown. Virus has not been isolated from the semen or urethra after primary infection.

Females

Recurrent infection in females may be so minor or hidden from view in the vagina or cervix that it is unnoticed. This may explain why some males with primary disease are not aware of the source. Only 22% of women with culture or serologic evidence of genital HSV infection report a history of genital ulcers.

Prevention

Virus can be recovered from the eroded lesions for about 5 days after the onset, but sexual contact should be avoided until reepithelialization is complete. Condoms (rubber, not natural membranes) should be used by patients with a history of recurrent genital herpes. For sexual partners who have both had genital herpes, protective measures are probably not necessary if both carry the same virus type (one partner infected the other) and active lesions are not present. Having herpes in one area does not protect one from acquiring the infection in another location (Fig 31). Contact should be avoided when active lesions are present.

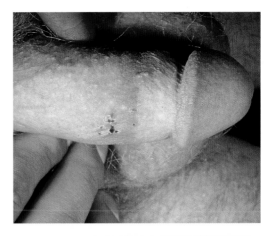

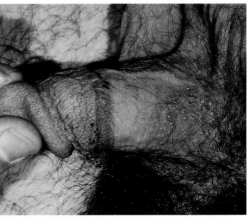

Fig 31.—Recurrent herpes simplex. Simultaneous presence of resolving lesions that have formed crusts and a new area of vesicles at another site.

Genital Herpes Simplex During Pregnancy

Infants of mothers exposed to herpes simplex virus during pregnancy and in whom a primary infection then develops are at greater risk for morbidity and death than infants of women who had herpes before pregnancy and then experienced a recurrence.[8]

Primary infection

During the first 20 weeks of gestation

Primary infection is associated with an increased frequency of spontaneous abortion, stillbirth, and congenital malformations.[9,10] However, most infants whose mothers have a primary infection during the first or second trimester are healthy.

During the third trimester

The rate of complications for the fetus is greater than 40% when infection occurs during the third trimester.[11] These include aborted pregnancy, premature labor, or transmission of infection to the infant either in utero or at delivery. When several weeks have elapsed between the primary first episode and delivery, intrauterine growth retardation may be observed.

Management

The risk that the neonate will acquire an HSV infection is high if a woman is experiencing her first attack of genital HSV infection around the time of delivery. Under such conditions, cesarean delivery should be considered. The risk for the neonate is low if infection occurs during the first, second, or early third trimester. Mothers are followed and managed according to circumstances at the time of delivery.

Recurrent infection

The risk of symptomatic neonatal HSV infection after vaginal delivery in a woman with known recurrent genital HSV infection is very low.

Management

Women with a history of genital HSV infection who have no symptoms at the onset of labor should be advised that the risk of exposure to excreted HSV is low and that, even if inadvertent exposure occurs, the risk that the neonate will acquire an HSV infection is less than 8%.[12] Vaginal delivery is reasonable for women who have a history of genital herpes but who have no signs of symptoms of recurrence at the onset of labor. Exposure of infants to HSV should be avoided by cesarean delivery if the mother has herpetic lesions in the genital area at the onset of labor.

Neonatal Herpes Simplex Virus Infection

Neonatal infection is serious but rare. The mortality rate is about 50% in the absence of therapy; and many survivors have ocular or neurologic complications. Most infected neonates are exposed to the virus during vaginal delivery, but infection occurs in utero in many cases.

Risk

Infants born to women who have an active primary HSV infection have a risk of acquiring an infection of about 50%.

Presenting symptoms

Clinical signs of neonatal infection are usually present between the first and the seventh day of life. Presenting symptoms are neurologic in 79% of cases, cutaneous in 30%, respiratory in 19%, cyanosis/pallor/grayish skin in 16%, irritability in 12%, and fever in 7%.[13]

Clinical course

Progression to systemic infection from isolated skin vesicles can occur in a matter of days. The infection can be limited to the skin, eyes, or mouth, or can affect the central nervous system (CNS) or visceral organs, causing hepatitis, pneumonitis, intravascular coagulopathy, or encephalitis. Death is unusual when disease is limited to the skin but occurs in 15% to 50% of cases of brain and disseminated disease.[14]

Laboratory diagnosis

Herpes simplex virus is detected most early and frequently in pharyngeal swabs (in one third of infants on postnatal days 2 to 5). Cerebrospinal fluid (CSF) contains an increased amount of protein or pleocytosis or both in 72% of infected infants.

Herpes Simplex Encephalitis

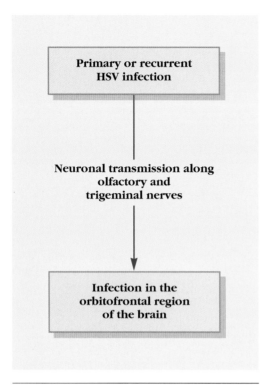

Primary or recurrent HSV infection

↓

Neuronal transmission along olfactory and trigeminal nerves

↓

Infection in the orbitofrontal region of the brain

Fig 32.—Herpes simplex encephalitis. Possible mechanism of infection.

Herpes simplex virus infections of the central nervous system are severe. Without therapy the mortality rate exceeds 70% and only about 9% rate of surviving patients return to normal. Herpes simplex encephalitis (HSE) occurs in approximately 1 in 250,000 to 1 in 500,000 individuals per year and is the most common cause of acute, sporadic viral encephalitis in the United States. HSE occurs throughout the year and in patients of all ages. Immunocompromise plays no apparent role.[15]

Pathogenesis

The CNS may be prone to HSV infection because intraneuronal spread may protect the virus from the immune system. Both primary and recurrent HSV infections can cause HSE. Primary infection is more common in children and young adults.

The major routes of access of virus to the CNS in primary infection are believed to be the olfactory and trigeminal nerves (Fig 32). The anatomical distribution of nerves from the olfactory tract along the inferomedial portion of the temporal lobe provides one possible neurologic avenue for viral access to the CNS and results in localization of the infection in the orbitofrontal region of the brain. Reactivation of virus peripherally in the olfactory bulb or the trigeminal ganglion, with subsequent neuronal transmission to the CNS, is another proposed mechanism of infection.

Clinical presentation

The clinical findings are nonspecific. The diagnosis should be suspected in patients who present with fever and altered mental status, although fever is absent in about 10% of cases. A flu-like syndrome with headache, myalgia, malaise, and upper respiratory symptoms may precede the onset of neurologic complaints (Fig 33). HSE then begins abruptly with local and diffuse cerebral dysfunction. The most common symptoms are severe headache, alteration in behavior, decreasing levels of consciousness, focal neurologic findings, and focal or generalized convulsions. Focal and generalized seizures occur in approximately two thirds of all patients. Motor paralyses are sometimes present. Patients without fever who present with personality changes may be seen by a psychiatrist.

Diagnosis

Cerebrospinal fluid examination

CSF examination is the most important diagnostic test. The pressure is normal or slightly elevated. The CSF shows a mononuclear pleocytosis with 50 to 300 leukocytes per microliter. Polymorphonuclear leukocytes may predominate in the early days of the disease; a number of red cells may be present. The protein is mildly elevated and the glucose level is usually normal. HSV is rarely isolated from the CSF; culturing from any other source is irrelevant in cases of HSE.

Newly developed assays of HSV antigens and viral DNA in CSF are used in many centers to make an early diagnosis. The CSF reveals antigens to HSV as early as 5 days after disease onset in 65% to 75% of cases. The assay is nearly 100% specific and increases in sensitivity as the disease progresses. Polymerase chain-reaction assays are used to detect evidence of viral DNA in the CSF.[16,17] This test can confirm the diagnosis in 1 or 2 days after the onset of neurologic symptoms.

Electroencephalography (EEG)

Characteristic EEG findings include spike and slow-wave activity that arise from the temporal lobe. Early in the course of the disease, abnormal electrical activity usually involves one temporal lobe. It then spreads, in 7 to 10 days, to the contralateral temporal lobe.

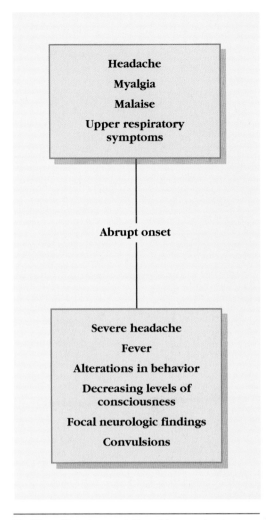

Fig 33.—Clinical presentation of herpes simplex encephalitis.

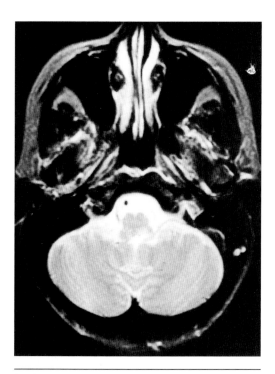

Fig 34.—Herpes simplex encephalitis in patient with leukemia. MR scan shows parapontine lesions.

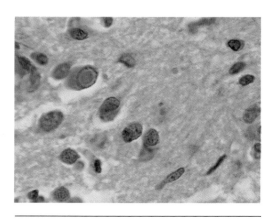

Fig 35.—Brain biopsy shows diffuse necrosis of brain tissue with eosinophilic nuclear inclusions.

Imaging

Computerized tomographic scanning is insensitive in detecting early HSE.[12] Magnetic resonance (MR) imaging is the most valuable imaging test for the diagnosis of HSE (Fig 34). Increased signals, particularly on T2-weighted sequences, are seen in the temporal lobes, inferior frontal regions, insulae, and cingulate gyri. These are often bilateral.

Brain biopsy

Brain biopsy is the most sensitive and specific diagnostic method (Fig 35); however, many neurologists object to biopsy because of its risks. An early diagnosis of HSE can be made in most cases on the bases of clinical findings and with the use of newer laboratory tests. The complication rate for brain biopsy is approximately 3%. Acute complications at biopsy include poorly controlled cerebral edema and hemorrhage (because of poor tissue visualization). The long-term complication of seizure disorders is uncommon.

Polymerase chain reaction

Polymerase chain reaction is a rapid and noninvasive technique for the diagnosis of HSE.[18-20] The diagnosis can be made in 4 to 6 hours by detecting specific virus DNA fragments present in CSF. These fragments can be identified only a few hours after the infection begins.

Serology

The majority of adult patients are seropositive for HSV prior to their illness; therefore, seroconversion is usually not seen. A fourfold or greater rise in CSF antibodies occurs in the month after onset of infection and is not helpful in making an early diagnosis.

Pathology

The gross appearance of the brain shows acute inflammation, congestion, and softening, usually asymmetrically centered around the temporal lobes, but also involving adjacent areas. Petechiae or larger hemorrhages are the acute changes; necrosis and liquefaction occur in about 2 weeks.

Herpes Simplex Esophagitis

The esophagus is the visceral organ most frequently infected by HSV. Herpes simplex esophagitis occurs in patients with impaired cell-mediated immunity, especially those with acquired immunodeficiency syndrome (AIDS). It is rare in immunocompetent patients. The disease probably goes unrecognized in many patients; symptoms of pain are often attributed to peptic ulcer. The infection may originate from an oropharyngeal HSV infection, but this has not been proven.

Etiology

The etiology is unknown. Most HSV isolates are HSV-1. The infection may be acquired by oral contact, from direct extension of oropharyngeal HSV infection into the esophagus, or by reactivation of HSV, and is spread to the esophageal mucosa via the vagus nerve. Trauma to tissues (eg, gastroesophageal reflux, esophageal instrumentation, or nasogastric drainage) may predispose to infection. Patients with intermittent recurrent esophageal symptoms could have recurrent disease, but this has not been proven.

Clinical presentation

The distal esophagus is most commonly involved. Painful swallowing, sensation of obstruction, fever, substernal chest pain, and weight loss are the most common symptoms.[21] Evidence of HSV infection elsewhere is usually lacking. Assessment of immunocompetence is recommended in all patients. This disease entity is probably not as rare as the scarcity of reports suggests, but is just frequently unrecognized.

Laboratory studies

Endoscopy

Endoscopy is the diagnostic procedure of choice. Esophagoscopy with biopsy or collection of aspirate for cytologic examination and culture are required to make a definitive diagnosis. Endoscopic examination reveals erythema and multiple oval, punched-out ulcers, with or without exudate, in the distal and/or mid-esophagus (Figs 36 and 37). Coalescence of ulcers can lead to diffuse erosive esophagitis. Candida infection, cytomegalovirus infection, and peptic esophagitis have the same appearance; therefore, a biopsy specimen or aspirate for cytologic examination and culture is essential for definitive diagnosis.

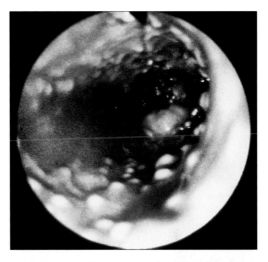

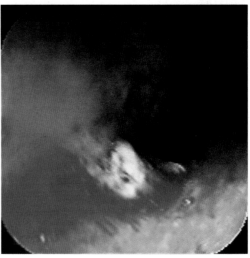

Fig 36.—Herpes simplex virus esophagitis. Endoscopic examination reveals oval, punched-out ulcers with exudate.

Fig 37.—Herpes simplex virus esophagitis. The esophagus shows multiple oval, punched-out ulcers over the entire surface. In most cases the ulcers are localized to the distal and/or mid-esophagus.

Contrast studies

Single-contrast studies cannot provide a specific diagnosis even when esophagitis is present.[22] Ulcers may be demonstrated with double-contrast studies, but these procedures may not be well tolerated because most patients have severe pain with swallowing.

Histology and cytology

Biopsies are obtained from the edge of the ulcer. Biopsies and cytology specimens show the same changes. Inflammation is always present. The changes are the same as those found in cutaneous herpes infection. There is ballooning, degeneration, "ground-glass" change in the nuclei, and eosinophilic intranuclear inclusions with or without multinucleated giant cells. HSV can be identified with immunohistochemical stains and with electron microscopy.

Culture

Culture specimens from the esophagus are almost always positive for HSV unless antiviral therapy has been started.

Serology and immune studies

Most HSV isolates are type 1. A fourfold or greater rise in HSV antibody titers can be demonstrated.

Herpes Simplex Hepatitis

Herpes simplex hepatitis is a rare disease with nonspecific symptoms. The disease may be rapidly fatal, and the diagnosis is often not made until just before death or at autopsy. A high index of suspicion in the appropriate setting is important to make an early diagnosis.

Neonates may develop liver infection during dissemination of a herpes infection acquired from the mother during birth. Adult HSV hepatitis is most frequently seen in patients who are immunocompromised, especially solid-organ or bone marrow transplant recipients, patients receiving steroid therapy, or healthy women in the third trimester of pregnancy.

HSV hepatitis in adults may be due either to primary infection or to reactivation of a latent infection. A review of the literature in 1987 revealed 35 cases of HSV hepatitis in adults. Most were immunocompromised and eight (23%) had pregnancy as their only risk factor. Thirty (86%) of the 35 patients died of the disease, including four of the eight pregnant women.[23]

Clinical presentation

The spectrum of severity of HSV hepatitis is broad. Mild, transient elevations in levels of serum aminotransferases are seen in patients with both primary and recurrent genital HSV infection. Children who die with disseminated HSV infection have fulminant hepatitis. HSV hepatitis usually occurs during disseminated infection of other organs or tissues in marrow and solid-organ transplant recipients.

The course of HSV hepatitis is rapid and is characterized by severe abdominal pain, fever, CNS manifestations, and renal dysfunction. Icteric and anicteric presentations are seen.

Some patients present with an acute viral-like syndrome consistent with primary HSV infection—malaise, myalgias, chills, and, in some cases, upper respiratory symptoms and headache. Mucocutaneous lesions are not always present; the absence of skin lesions may delay the diagnosis.

Marrow transplant patients

HSV hepatitis is a rare complication among patients undergoing marrow transplantation. Allogeneic marrow transplantation requires immunosuppressive therapy before and after transplantation.[24]

Solid-organ transplant patients

In one report, the overall frequency of HSV hepatitis was 0.3% in 3536 patients undergoing liver, kidney, and heart transplant operations.[25] Twelve patients developed HSV hepatitis a median of 18 days after solid-organ transplantation.

Pregnant women

Although very rare, HSV hepatitis can occur in otherwise healthy women in their third trimester of pregnancy.[26] Pregnant women have alterations in humoral and cell-mediated immunity to prevent rejection of the antigenically foreign fetus and placenta. These changes include inversion of the B/T lymphocyte ratio, T-cell subset abnormalities, and decreased natural killer-cell activity. The alterations in cell-mediated immunity may be responsible for the increased susceptibility to viral illness.

Laboratory studies

Abnormal laboratory findings at the time of diagnosis may include elevated liver enzymes (serum aspartate aminotransferase and serum alanine aminotransferase), disseminated intravascular coagulation, thrombocytopenia (<100,000 platelets/mL), increased percentage of band forms, and abnormal chest radiograph (pleural effusion, atelectasis, consolidation). Elevations in bilirubin levels are usually moderate. Diagnosis can be made by light microscopy aided by electron microscopy, immunohistochemistry, and viral cultures of liver tissue. Serotyping in reported cases revealed both types 1 and 2 in equal numbers. The laboratory abnormalities that are common in patients who die are a low platelet count, a high percentage of band forms, prolonged partial thromboplastin time (but not prolonged prothrombin time), and a high creatinine level.

Immunohistochemical studies

Positive staining is seen primarily within the nuclei but also demonstrates antigen in the cytoplasm and cell membrane of affected hepatocytes (but none in the areas of necrosis).

Histology

Microscopically, there are two patterns of necrosis and inflammation in the liver: focal and diffuse. The two patterns may represent different degrees of severity or different responses in individual patients.

Focal pattern. The focal pattern shows multiple, small foci of coagulative necrosis infiltrated by neutrophils and scattered randomly throughout the lobules. Areas of confluence may be present. Many portal areas are spared. The smaller foci have rounded outlines; the larger areas are more geographic. Hepatocytes with "ground-glass" nuclei may be present at the periphery of the necrotic areas. These inclusions are intensely eosinophilic and homogeneous.

Diffuse pattern. The diffuse pattern shows extensive inflammation of the portal zone. Broad areas of necrosis are surrounded by a zone in which hepatocytes contain either "ground-glass" intranuclear inclusions or eosinophilic Cowdry type A intranuclear inclusion bodies.

Herpes Simplex Pneumonitis

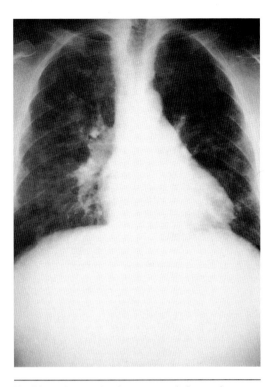

Fig 38.—Herpes simplex pneumonia in a patient with acute leukemia. The interstitial pattern is typical of herpetic pneumonia.

HSV pneumonitis is rare and occurs almost exclusively in immunocompromised patients.[27] Dissemination of virus from primary or recurrent oral or cutaneous lesions may produce a bilateral interstitial pneumonitis (Fig 38). HSV infection of the lower respiratory tract occurs from extension of active herpetic lesions from the trachea or bronchus into lung parenchyma, causing a focal necrotizing pneumonitis. Bacterial, fungal, and parasitic infections are common in HSV pneumonitis. The mortality of HSV pneumonia in untreated immunocompromised patients is greater than 80%. Lung biopsy is required for diagnosis since other opportunistic pathogens such as cytomegalovirus can also cause interstitial pneumonia.

Varicella-Zoster Virus Infection

Two syndromes occur from infection with herpes virus varicellae (varicella-zoster virus [VZV]): varicella (chickenpox) and herpes zoster (shingles). Chickenpox is the primary infection and usually occurs in childhood. The virus becomes latent in nerve ganglia and may be reactivated years later to produce herpes zoster.

Latency and reactivation

Following acute VZV, the virus becomes latent in dorsal root ganglia cells. Years later it may be reactivated by stress or any immunocompromising condition, such as Hodgkin's disease, AIDS, and cancer chemotherapy, and replicate in the dorsal root ganglia. Virions then migrate through the axon to the skin of a single dermatome or a small number of contiguous dermatomes to produce shingles.[28]

Eruptive phase

The extent of involvement varies. The disease may go unnoticed in young children; older children and adults have a more extensive eruption. The rash begins on the trunk (centripetal distribution) and spreads to the face and extremities (Fig 41). A scarlatiniform or morbilliform erythema may precede

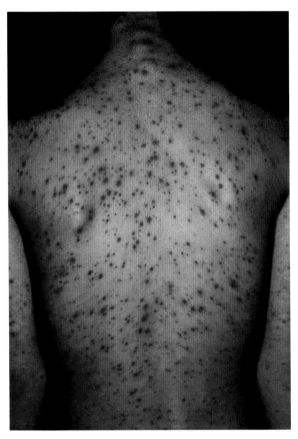

A. The rash begins on the trunk (centripetal distribution).

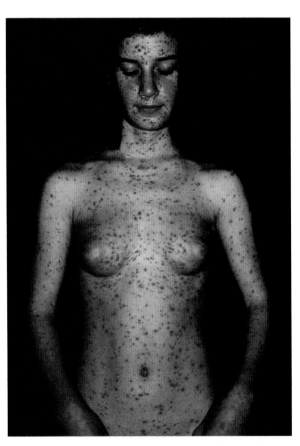

B. In older children and adults more extensive eruption occurs and numerous lesions spread to the face and extremities.

Fig 41.—Chickenpox. The distribution.

Varicella-Zoster Virus Infection

Two syndromes occur from infection with herpes virus varicellae (varicella-zoster virus [VZV]): varicella (chickenpox) and herpes zoster (shingles). Chickenpox is the primary infection and usually occurs in childhood. The virus becomes latent in nerve ganglia and may be reactivated years later to produce herpes zoster.

Latency and reactivation

Following acute VZV, the virus becomes latent in dorsal root ganglia cells. Years later it may be reactivated by stress or any immunocompromising condition, such as Hodgkin's disease, AIDS, and cancer chemotherapy, and replicate in the dorsal root ganglia. Virions then migrate through the axon to the skin of a single dermatome or a small number of contiguous dermatomes to produce shingles.[28]

Chickenpox (Varicella)

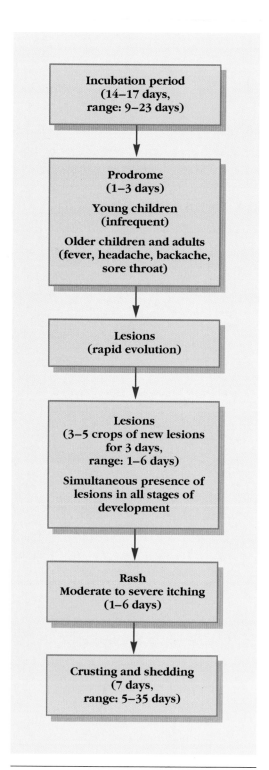

Incubation period
(14–17 days,
range: 9–23 days)

↓

Prodrome
(1–3 days)

Young children
(infrequent)

Older children and adults
(fever, headache, backache,
sore throat)

↓

Lesions
(rapid evolution)

↓

Lesions
(3–5 crops of new lesions
for 3 days,
range: 1–6 days)

Simultaneous presence of
lesions in all stages of
development

↓

Rash
Moderate to severe itching
(1–6 days)

↓

Crusting and shedding
(7 days,
range: 5–35 days)

Fig 39.—Chickenpox (varicella). The evolution of signs and symptoms.

Epidemiology and etiology

Incidence

Chickenpox is a common, highly contagious illness. Approximately 3 million cases occur each year in the United States.

Age

Over 90% of cases occur in children less than 12 years of age; 10% of the population over the age of 15 remain susceptible. Most urban children are infected before puberty. Subclinical infections occur.

Transmission

The disease is acquired by inhalation of virus-containing particles from droplets from the nasopharynx of an infected individual. These cause an initial infection in the respiratory epithelium. Skin vesicles contain virus but are not the primary source. Scabs are not infectious. Patients are contagious from 2 days before onset of the rash until all lesions have crusted.

Evolution of disease

The virus disseminates to distant cells of the reticuloendothelial system and, finally, viremia leads to infection of the skin. Infection may occur in all viscera, but clinical appreciation of this event is usually limited to immunocompromised patients.

Season

The virus is endemic but becomes epidemic during late winter and spring.

Immunity

Lasting immunity follows recovery. Second attacks are rare even in the immunocompromised.

Clinical course

Incubation period

The incubation period is 14 to 17 days (Fig 39). The incubation period is shorter than 14 days in the immunocompromised patient.

Prodrome

The prodromal symptoms in children are absent or low-grade. Older children and adults experience fever (1 to 6 days), headache, backache, and sore throat.

Fever

The fever varies from 101°F to 105°F and returns to normal when the vesicles have disappeared.

Symptoms

Moderate to intense pruritus is usually present during the vesicular stage.

Lesions

Vesicle

The lesion starts as a 2-mm to 4-mm red papule, which develops an irregular outline (rose petal) as a thin-walled clear vesicle appears on the surface (dew drop). This lesion, "dew drop on a rose petal," is highly characteristic (Fig 40,A).

Pustule

The vesicle becomes umbilicated (depressed in the center) and cloudy, has an irregular (scalloped) border, and breaks in 8 to 12 hours (Fig 40,B).

Crust

The lesion dries to form a crust as the red base disappears (Fig 40,C). Secondary infection or excoriation extends the process into the dermis, producing a crater-like scar.

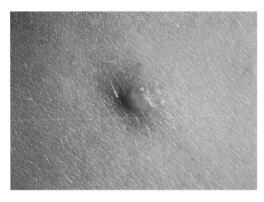

A. A thin-walled vesicle with clear fluid forms on a red base.

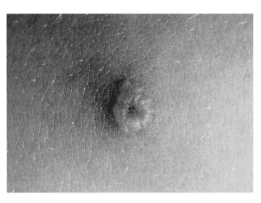

B. The vesicle becomes cloudy and depressed in the center (umbilicated), with an irregular (scalloped) border.

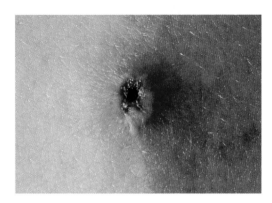

C. A crust forms in the center and eventually replaces the remaining portion of the vesicle at the periphery.

Fig 40.—The evolution of chickenpox lesions.

Eruptive phase

The extent of involvement varies. The disease may go unnoticed in young children; older children and adults have a more extensive eruption. The rash begins on the trunk (centripetal distribution) and spreads to the face and extremities (Fig 41). A scarlatiniform or morbilliform erythema may precede

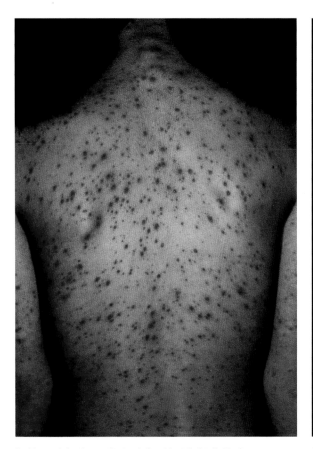

A. The rash begins on the trunk (centripetal distribution).

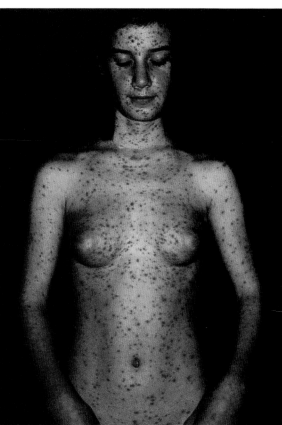

B. In older children and adults more extensive eruption occurs and numerous lesions spread to the face and extremities.

Fig 41.—Chickenpox. The distribution.

the classic eruption. Lesions of different stages are present at the same time (Fig 42). New lesion formation ceases by day 3 and most crusting occurs by day 6. Vesicles often form in the oral cavity and vagina and rupture quickly to form multiple, aphthae-like ulcers. Immunocompromised patients have a longer course.

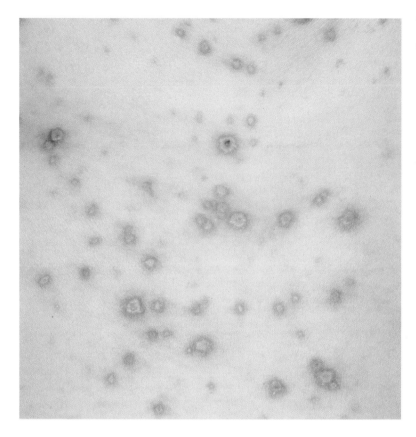

Fig 42.—Chickenpox. Lesions of different stages.

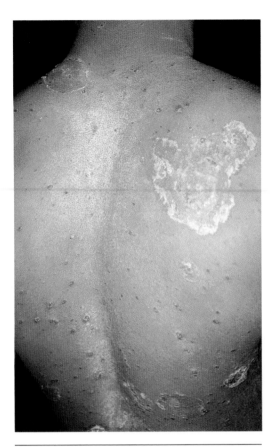

Fig 43.—Chickenpox. Bacterial skin infection is a common complication in children. An impetigo-like pattern of infection is the most common presentation.

Complications

The disease is usually uneventful in healthy individuals. Chickenpox in the immunocompromised patient is associated with significant morbidity and mortality. Complications occur most often in children with leukemia, lymphoma, or solid tumors.

Skin infection

The most common complication in children is bacterial skin infection. Secondary infection is suspected when large, moist, denuded areas appear, expand in area, and become painful. An impetigo-like pattern is a common presentation (Fig 43).

Scarring

Scarring occurs frequently, especially in older children and adults. Round, deep, punched-out scars, "pock marks," are a disfiguring complication resulting from extension of the vesicle into the dermis. Self-inflicted trauma to the crusts (picking) can also extend the process into the dermis, but most scars occur from lesions that were never manipulated. During the healing process a thick crust adheres to the base of the resolving lesion and will eventually heal with scarring (Fig 44). These disfiguring scars are permanent, but do show some improvement with time. The extent and severity of scarring cannot be predicted from the severity of the disease.

Neurologic

Cerebellar ataxia, encephalitis, and Reye's syndrome are the most common complications.

Encephalitis. Encephalitis in an otherwise healthy patient occurs in less than 1 per 1000 cases. Complete recovery occurs in over 80% of individuals. Encephalitis occurs in 6% of immunocompromised patients. There are two forms of encephalitis. The cerebellar form seen in children is self-limited, and complete recovery occurs. The symptoms include ataxia with nystagmus, headache, nausea, vomiting, and nuchal rigidity. Adult encephalitis patients have altered sensorium, seizures, and focal neurologic signs with a mortality rate of up to 35%.

Reye's syndrome. Reye's syndrome is an acute, noninflammatory encephalopathy associated with hepatitis or fatty metamorphosis of the liver; 20% to 30% of Reye's syndrome cases are preceded by varicella. The fatality rate is 20%. Salicylates used during the varicella infection may increase the risk of developing Reye's syndrome.

Pneumonia

Pneumonia is rare in immunocompetent children, but is the most common serious complication in such adults. Over 25% of children with leukemia may develop varicella-zoster viral pneumonia. Pneumonia develops 1 to 6 days after onset of the rash. In most cases it is asymptomatic and can only be detected by a chest x-ray examination. Symptoms include cough, dyspnea, fever, and chest pain. Fatalities are rare.

Hepatitis

Hepatitis occurs in nearly 20% of immunocompromised children. It is the most common complication in immunocompromised patients.

Thrombocytopenia

Mild degrees of thrombocytopenia can accompany routine cases. Thrombocytopenic purpura is rare. It begins on the fifth to the tenth day. Recovery occurs spontaneously after 3 to 4 months.

Immune response

IgG, IgM, and IgA antibodies appear 2 to 5 days after the onset of the rash, and their levels peak during the second and third weeks. Thereafter, the titers gradually fall, although IgG persists at low levels. If zoster occurs later, the levels of these antibodies increase rapidly and become much higher than during the primary infection. These antibodies seem to have an incomplete protective effect: varicella is not severe in children with α-gammaglobulinaemia; and, while maternal or administered antibody reduces the severity of infection, it does not prevent it.

A. Round, deep, punched-out scars ("pock marks") are a disfiguring, permanent complication.

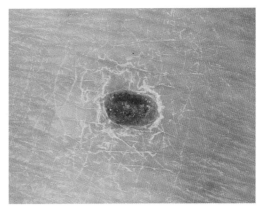

B. A thick crust adheres to the base of this resolving lesion, which will eventually heal with scarring.

Fig 44.—Chickenpox. Scarring.

Chickenpox in the immunocompromised patient

Patients with cancer or patients who are taking immunosuppressive drugs, particularly systemic corticosteroids, have extensive eruptions and more complications. The potential for nosocomial transmission with primary varicella and herpes zoster should be kept in mind, particularly in wards where a high proportion of patients are immunocompromised. The mortality rate for immunocompromised children or children with leukemia is 7% to 14%. Adults with malignancy and varicella have a mortality rate as high as 50%.

Hemorrhagic chickenpox

Hemorrhagic chickenpox, also called malignant chickenpox, is a serious complication (Fig 45).

Lesions. The lesions are numerous, often bullous, and bleeding occurs in the skin at the base of the lesion. The bullae turn dark brown and then black as blood accumulates in the blister fluid.

Systemic symptoms. Patients are usually toxic, have high fever and delirium, and may develop convulsions and coma. They frequently bleed from the gastrointestinal tract and mucous membranes. Pneumonia with hemoptysis commonly occurs.

Mortality rate. The mortality rate is as high as 70%.[29]

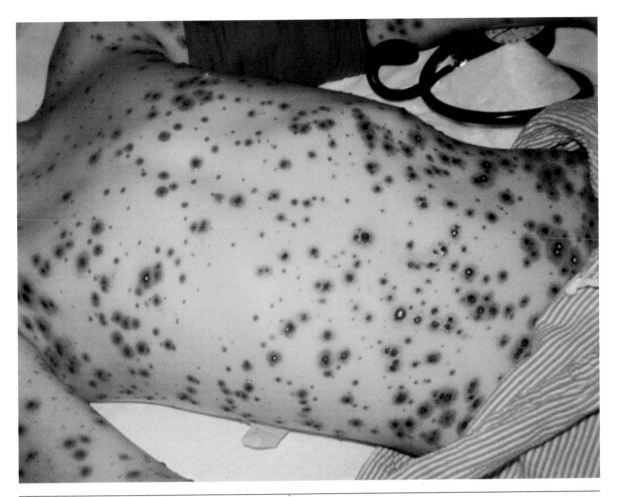

Fig 45.—Hemorrhagic chickenpox. Numerous vesicular and bullous lesions with hemorrhage at the base. This rare complication occurs in immunocompromised children.

Chickenpox during pregnancy

Varicella during pregnancy poses a risk for both the mother and the unborn child. Pregnant women may have systemic complications such as pneumonia. Smoking is a possible risk factor.

First trimester

Women who acquire chickenpox during the early months of pregnancy may deliver a child with multiple congenital anomalies (congenital varicella syndrome). This syndrome is so rare that accurate rates of fetal infection during maternal infection have not been established. Therefore, parents can only be informed that fetal damage is possible if the mother is infected during the early months of pregnancy.

Second trimester

Maternal varicella in the middle months of pregnancy may result in undetected fetal chickenpox. The newborn child who has already had chickenpox is at risk for developing herpes zoster (shingles). This may explain why some infants and children develop herpes zoster without the expected history of chickenpox.

Near birth

The time of onset of maternal lesions correlates directly with the frequency and severity of neonatal disease (Fig 46).[30,31]

2 to 3 weeks before delivery. If the mother has varicella 2 to 3 weeks before delivery, the fetus may be infected in utero and be born with or develop lesions 1 to 4 days after birth. Transplacental maternal antibody protects the infant and the course is usually benign.

5 days before to 2 days after delivery. A high rate of disseminated varicella in the infant is observed when the mother's eruption appears 1 to 5 days before delivery, or within 2 days after delivery. The child's eruption

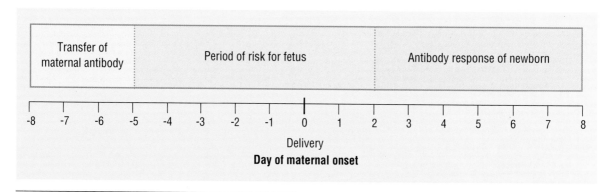

Fig 46.—Varicella in newborns. For neonates, the risk of varicella infection and its associated complications is greatest when maternal onset of disease occurs in a 7-day period from 5 days before delivery to 2 days after delivery. (Adapted from Straus SE, et al. *Ann Intern Med.* 1988;108:221-237.)

will appear 5 to 10 days after birth. When the rash appears in infants between 5 and 10 days old, the mortality rate may be as high as 20%. In this situation, the virus is either acquired transplacentally or from contact with maternal lesions during birth; there is insufficient time to receive adequate maternal antibody. These infants should be given zoster immune globulin (ZIG), varicella-zoster immune globulin (VZIG), or gamma globulin (if ZIG or VZIG are not available).

More than 2 days after delivery. Maternal infection that develops more than 2 days after delivery is associated with onset of disease in a newborn approximately 2 weeks later, at which point the immune system is better able to respond to the infection.

Laboratory diagnosis

Culture
In questionable cases, virus can be cultured from vesicular fluid.

Serologic testing
The main value of serologic testing is the assessment of immune status in immunocompromised patients (such as children with neoplastic diseases) who are at risk of developing severe disease with VZV infection.

Quantitative tests. The quantitative test measures IgG and IgM antibodies. The presence of IgM antibodies or a fourfold or greater rise in paired sera IgG titer indicates recent infection. The presence of IgG indicates past exposure and immunity.

Qualitative tests. The qualitative screening test uses the same method, but IgG is measured at only a single dilution (1:10).

Tzanck smear
This cytologic smear (described for the diagnosis of herpes simplex) is a valuable tool for rapid diagnosis. The test does not differentiate between herpes simplex and varicella.

Chest x-ray
A chest x-ray examination should be obtained if respiratory symptoms develop.

Polymerase chain reaction
Varicella-zoster virus DNA can be detected by the polymerase chain reaction technique. It is a useful laboratory tool for the early diagnosis of VZV–associated neurological disease.[32] Virus has been demonstrated in the CSF of patients with herpes zoster meningitis.[33] An early diagnosis of varicella in adults can be made by demonstrating virus DNA in respiratory epithelial cells and in peripheral blood leukocytes.[34]

Herpes Zoster

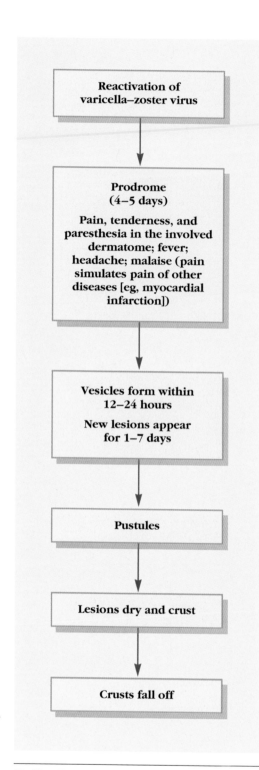

**Reactivation of
varicella–zoster virus**

↓

**Prodrome
(4–5 days)**

**Pain, tenderness, and
paresthesia in the involved
dermatome; fever;
headache; malaise (pain
simulates pain of other
diseases [eg, myocardial
infarction])**

↓

**Vesicles form within
12–24 hours**

**New lesions appear
for 1–7 days**

↓

Pustules

↓

Lesions dry and crust

↓

Crusts fall off

Fig 47.—The clinical course of herpes zoster.

Herpes zoster, or shingles, is a cutaneous viral infection that results from reactivation of varicella-zoster virus that has been dormant in the dorsal root ganglia (Fig 47). It generally involves the skin of a single dermatome (Fig 48). There are usually three phases: the prodromal phase, the acute phase (vesicular phase), and the chronic phase (postherpetic neuralgia). Not every patient passes through each phase, and some patients have unusual or atypical presentations. An attack of herpes zoster does not confer lasting immunity, but recurrence is rare. There is no seasonal variation or relation to epidemics of chickenpox. The potential for nosocomial transmission of the virus from patients with herpes zoster should be kept in mind, particularly in wards where a high proportion of patients are immunocompromised. Recurrent herpes zoster infections may be an early indicator of HIV disease. It is a frequent precursor of AIDS.

Zoster during pregnancy

Herpes zoster during pregnancy, whether it occurs early or late in the pregnancy, appears to have no deleterious effects on either the mother or the infant.

Epidemiology and etiology

Age

Persons of all ages are afflicted. Herpes zoster occurs in young individuals, but the incidence increases with age. It occurs in 10% to 20% of all persons. There is an increased incidence of zoster in immunocompetent children who acquire chickenpox when younger than 2 months.

Etiology

Zoster results from reactivation of varicella virus that entered the cutaneous nerves during an earlier episode of chickenpox, traveled to the dorsal root ganglia, and remained in a latent form. The virus is reactivated and subsequently travels back down the sensory nerve, infecting the skin.

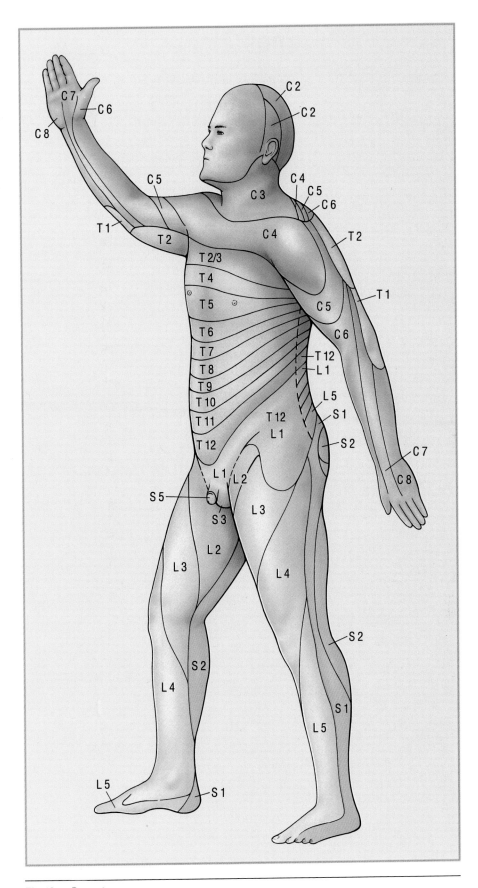

Fig 48.—Dermatome areas.

Risk factors

Age, immunosuppressive drugs, lymphoma, fatigue, emotional upsets, and radiation therapy have been implicated in reactivating the virus. Those affected may have acquired chickenpox by the transplacental route. Although reported, herpes zoster acquired by direct contact with a patient having active varicella or herpes zoster is rare. Some herpes zoster patients, particularly children, have no previous history of chickenpox. Following contact with such patients, infections are more inclined to result from reactivation of latent infection. Patients with herpes zoster are not more likely to have an underlying malignancy.[35] Herpes zoster frequently occurs in patients infected with the human immunodeficiency virus and is often the first clinical manifestation of AIDS.

Risk groups

The predisposition in the elderly for the development of herpes zoster is considered to be a consequence of diminishing immunologic function. Herpes zoster is clearly associated with immune suppression. Bone marrow and other transplant recipients, and persons with malignancies, especially lymphoreticular malignancies (eg, Hodgkin's disease) are at increased risk and demonstrate increased incidence of herpes zoster.[36,37] The elderly are also at greater risk in developing segmental pain, which can continue for months after the skin lesions have healed.

Transmission

Varicella-zoster virus can be cultured from vesicles during an eruption. It may also cause chickenpox in those not previously infected.

Clinical course

Prodrome

Preeruptive pain, itching, or burning, generally localized to the dermatome, precedes the eruption by 4 to 5 days. Prodromal symptoms may be absent, particularly in children. Segmental pain and constitutional symptoms gradually subside as the eruption appears.

Pain. The pain may simulate pleurisy, myocardial infarction, abdominal disease, or migraine headache, and presents a difficult diagnostic problem until the characteristic eruption provides the answer. "Zoster sine herpete" refers to segmental neuralgia without a cutaneous eruption and is rare.

Tenderness. Preeruptive tenderness or hyperesthesia throughout the dermatome is a useful predictive sign.

Other symptoms. Constitutional symptoms of fever, headache, and malaise may precede the eruption by several days. Regional lymphadenopathy may be present.

Duration

The duration varies from 2 to 5 weeks in immunocompetent patients. The elderly or debilitated patient may have a prolonged and difficult course. For them, the eruption is typically more extensive and inflammatory, occasionally resulting in hemorrhagic blisters, skin necrosis, secondary bacterial infection, or extensive scarring, which is sometimes hypertrophic or keloidal.

Similar to the elderly or debilitated patient, an immunocompromised patient usually has a more severe and fulminant course that frequently is prolonged for weeks to months. Importantly, immunocompromised patients develop disseminated herpes zoster more frequently and the dissemination may be to the skin, lungs, liver, gastrointestinal tract, or brain.

Chronic herpes zoster. Chronic herpes zoster has been reported in patients infected with the human immunodeficiency virus, especially when their CD4 lymphocyte counts are depressed. Depletion of CD4 lymphocytes is associated with more severe, chronic, and recurrent varicella-zoster virus infections. These lesions are typical at the onset but evolve into non-healing ulcers. Resistant strains of varicella-zoster virus are a common problem in patients with chronic herpes zoster.

Zoster-associated pain

Pain is the major cause of morbidity in herpes zoster.[38] The mechanism of pain has not been explained. Postherpetic neuralagia is a term that has been inconsistently defined. Zoster-associated pain has been used to describe the whole phenomenon of acute and chronic pain associated with herpes zoster infection. This does not imply that the acute and chronic pain are the same, merely that the continuum of zoster pain is being considered.

Incidence. There is an increasing incidence and duration of pain with age. The majority of patients under 30 years of age experience no pain. By age 40, the risk of prolonged pain lasting longer than 1 month increases to 33%. By age 70, the risk increases to 74%.

Duration. Pain can persist in a dermatome for months or years after the lesions have disappeared.

Characteristics. The pain is often severe, intractable, and exhausting. The skin is frequently extremely tender to touch (tactile allodynia) and the patient may go to extraordinary lengths in an effort to protect the diseased area from innocuous mechanical stimuli. Firm compression of the skin does not exacerbate pain and may even provide relief. The degree of pain is not related to the extent of involvement, nor to the number of vesicles, degree of inflammation, or fibrosis in peripheral nerves. The scarred skin is often hyposensitive to pinprick but hypersensitive to light touch.

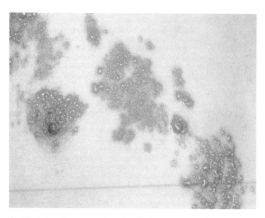

A. Vesicles of various sizes in clusters on an erythematous base.

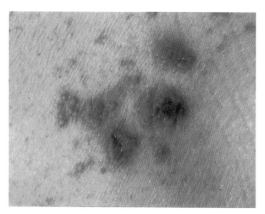

B. Cloudy umbilicated vesicles.

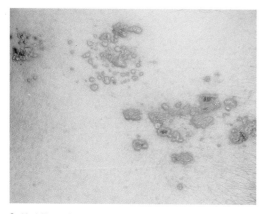

C. Umbilicated vesicles will form crusts.

Fig 49.—The evolution of herpes zoster lesions.

Evolution of lesions

Plaques

The eruption begins with red, swollen plaques of various sizes and spreads to involve part or all of a dermatome.

Vesicles

The vesicles arise in clusters from an erythematous base and become cloudy with purulent fluid and/or hemorrhagic by day 3 or 4 (Fig 49,A,B). The vesicles vary in size, in contrast to the cluster of uniformly sized vesicles noted in herpes simplex. Successive crops continue to appear for a period of 7 days.

Pustules and crusts

Vesicles either umbilicate or rupture before forming crusts in 7 to 10 days (Fig 49,C). These fall off in 14 to 21 days, often leaving residual hyperpigmentation or hypopigmented scarring.

Eruptive phase

Distribution. Possibly because chickenpox is centripetal (located on the trunk), the thoracic region is affected in two thirds of herpes zoster cases.

Localized. Although generally limited to the skin of a single dermatome, the eruption may involve one or two adjacent dermatomes (Fig 50). Occasionally, a few vesicles appear across the midline. Eruption is rare in bilaterally symmetrical or asymmetrical dermatomes.

Disseminated. Approximately 50% of patients with uncomplicated herpes zoster will have a viremia, with the appearance of 20 to 30 vesicles scattered over the skin surface outside the affected dermatome.

Eruptions in the immunocompromised patient

The extent and depth of inflammation is typically more severe in the immunocompromised patient (Fig 51). The vesicles may be larger and coalesce to form bullae. Also, there is more tissue destruction, with erosions as well as vesicles.

The lesions are more frequently erosive or ulcerative, with an entire dermatome affected rather than geographical areas. Because of the prolonged course, different phases may occur at the same time. Herpes zoster occurs with an increased frequency in areas of tissue damage such as those resulting from cutaneous metastatic disease or radiation therapy.

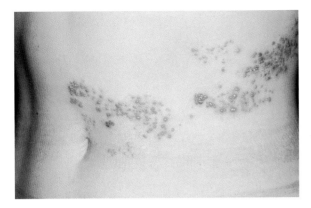

A. Classic presentation of groups of vesicles limited to a single dermatome in the thoracic region.

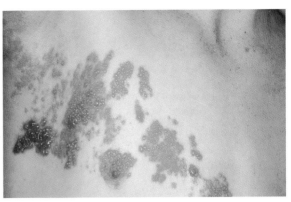

B. An extensive eruption of red, edematous plaques with vesicles involving almost the entire skin surface of a dermatome.

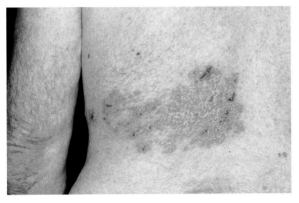

C. Vesicles have evolved into pustules in this huge plaque that involves more than one dermatome.

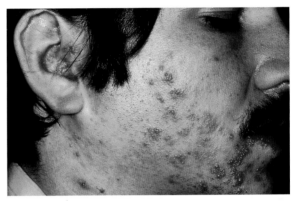

D. Unilateral single-dermatome distribution involving the mandibular branch of the fifth cranial nerve.

Fig 50.—Herpes zoster. Dermatome presentation.

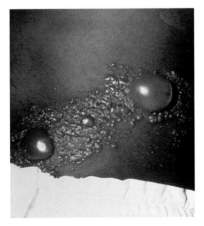

A. Severe infection in patient with insulin-dependent diabetes mellitus 15 months after renal transplantation.

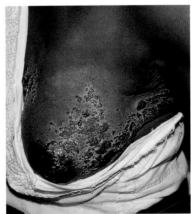

B. Painful infection in a 47-year-old woman following a lumpectomy and radiation therapy.

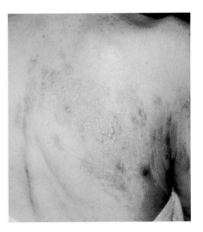

C. Herpes zoster infection in a 52-year-old woman 9 months after high-dose chemotherapy and bone marrow transplantation for breast cancer.

Fig 51.—Herpes zoster infections in immunocompromised patients.

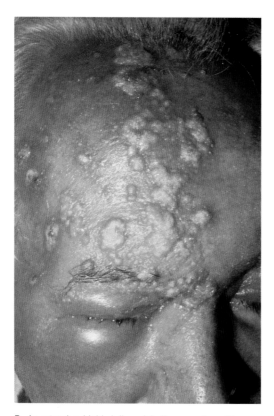

A. Involvement of the first branch of the fifth nerve. Vesicles present on the side of the nose are associated with the most serious ocular complications.

B. An extensive, highly inflamed, bullous eruption with edema of the orbital region.

Fig 52.—Herpes zoster (ophthalmic zoster).

Herpes zoster syndromes
Ophthalmic zoster

Definition
The fifth cranial, or trigeminal, nerve has three divisions: the ophthalmic, the maxillary, and the mandibular. The ophthalmic division further divides into three branches: the frontal, the lacrimal, and the nasociliary nerves. The frontal nerve separates into the supraorbital and supratrochlear nerves. Involvement of any branch of the trigeminal nerve is called herpes zoster ophthalmicus.

Incidence
Eight percent to 56% in various series.

Complications
Twenty percent to 72% of cases develop ocular complications (Table 1).

Distribution
The rash extends from eye level to the vertex of the skull, but does not cross the midline. Herpes zoster ophthalmicus may be confined to certain branches of the trigeminal nerve.

Hutchinson's sign
The tip and side of the nose and eye are innervated by the nasociliary branch of the trigeminal nerve. Vesicles on the side or tip of the nose (Hutchinson's sign) occurring during an episode of zoster are associated with the most serious ocular complications, including conjunctival, corneal, scleral, and other

ocular diseases, although this is not invariable (Fig 52,A). Involvement of the other sensory branches of the trigeminal nerve are most likely to yield periocular involvement but spare the eyeball (Fig 52,B).

Ramsay Hunt's syndrome

Definition

Varicella-zoster of the geniculate ganglion is called Ramsay Hunt's syndrome. There is involvement of the sensory portion and motor portion of the seventh cranial nerve.

Signs and symptoms

There may be unilateral loss of taste on the anterior two thirds of the tongue and vesicles on the tympanic membrane, external auditory meatus, concha, and pinna. Involvement of the motor division of the seventh cranial nerve causes unilateral facial paralysis. Auditory nerve involvement occurs in 40% of patients, resulting in hearing deficits and vertigo. Recovery from the motor paralysis is generally complete, but residual weakness is possible.

Sacral zoster

Signs and symptoms

A neurogenic bladder with urinary hesitancy or urinary retention has been reported to be associated with zoster of the T12, L1–L2, or S2–S4 dermatomes (Fig 53). Migration of virus to the adjacent autonomic nerves is responsible for these symptoms.

Table 1.— Ocular Complications in 86 Patients with Herpes Zoster Ophthalmicus*

Complication	No. of Patients
Lid involvement	11
Corneal involvement	66
Scleral involvement	4
Canalicular scarring	2
Uveitis	37
Glaucoma (secondary)	10
Persistent	2
Cataract	7
Neuro-ophthalmic involvement	7
Postherpetic neuralgia	15

*Some patients had more than one manifestation of involvement. (Adapted from Womack LW and Liesegang TJ. *Arch Ophthalmol.* 1983;101:44. By permission of the Mayo Foundation.)

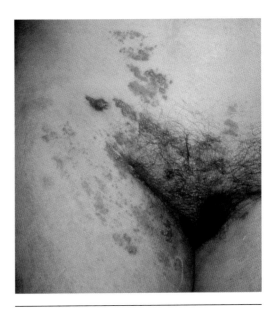

Fig 53.—Ilioinguinal and sacral zoster. Zoster of T12, L1-L2, or S2-S4 dermatomes can occasionally cause a neurogenic bladder. Acute urinary retention and polyuria are the most common symptoms.

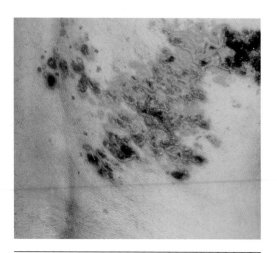

Fig 54.—Herpes zoster. The entire skin area of a dermatome is covered with vesicles. Secondary infection has increased the depth of involvement. Extensive scarring will follow (see Fig 55).

Complications

Motor paresis

Weakness in the muscle group associated with the infected dermatome may be observed before, during, or after an episode of herpes zoster. The weakness results from the spread of the virus from the dorsal root ganglia to the anterior root horn. Patients in the sixth to eighth decade of life are most commonly involved. Motor neuropathies are usually transient and about 75% of patients recover. They occur in about 5% of all cases of zoster but in up to 12% of patients with cephalic zoster. Ramsay Hunt's syndrome accounts for more than half of the cephalic motor neuropathies.

Necrosis, infection, and scarring

Elderly, malnourished, debilitated, or immunocompromised patients tend to have a more virulent and extensive course of disease. The entire skin area of a dermatome may be lost following diffuse vesiculation. Large adherent crusts promote infection and increase the depth of involvement (Fig 54). Scarring, sometimes hypertrophic or keloidal, will follow (Fig 55).

Encephalitis

Neurologic symptoms characteristically appear within the first 2 weeks after onset of the skin lesions (Fig 56). It is possible that encephalitis is immune-mediated rather than a result of viral invasion. Patients at greatest risk are those with trigeminal and disseminated herpes zoster as well as the immunocompromised. The mortality rate is 10% to 20%. Most survivors recover completely. Diagnosis is hampered by the fact that the virus is rarely isolated from the spinal fluid. Cell counts and protein concentration of the CSF are elevated in both encephalitis patients and in about 40% of typical herpes zoster patients.

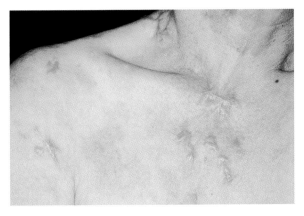

A. Keloidal scarring.

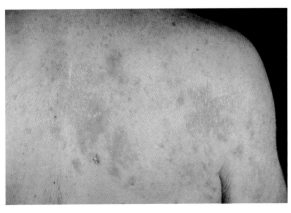

B. Superficial broad areas of scar tissue.

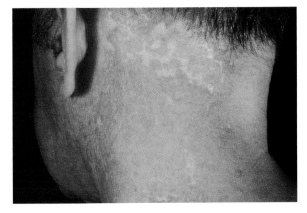

C. A group of depressed atrophic scars.

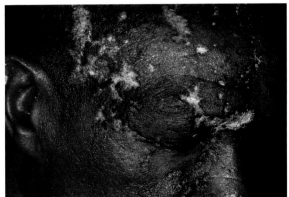

D. Residual scarring in an immunocompromised patient.

Fig 55.—Herpes zoster. Various patterns of scarring may occur.

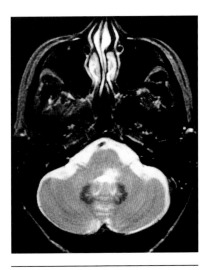

Fig 56.—Herpes zoster encephalitis in a 48-year-old patient who developed a seizure 9 months after a bone marrow transplant for non-Hodgkin's lymphoma.

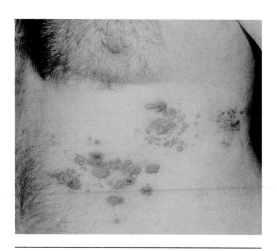

Fig 57.—Herpes zoster. A group of vesicles may be mistaken for poison ivy or herpes simplex. An elevated varicella-zoster virus IgM level confirms the diagnosis.

Differential diagnosis

Herpes simplex

Herpes simplex can be extensive, particularly on the trunk. It may be confined to a dermatome and possess many of the same features of herpes zoster (zosteriform herpes simplex). The vesicles of herpes zoster vary in size, while those of simplex are uniform within a cluster. Pain along the dermatome can help confirm herpes zoster; later recurrence will definitively confirm the diagnosis.

Poison ivy

A group of vesicles may be mistaken for poison ivy (Fig 57).

"Zoster sine herpete" (zoster without the rash)

Neuralgia within a dermatome without the typical rash can be confusing. A concurrent rise in varicella-zoster antibody titers has been demonstrated in a number of such cases.

Cellulitis

The eruption of herpes zoster may never evolve to the vesicular stage. The red, inflamed, edematous, or urticarial-like plaques may appear infected, but they usually have a fine, cobblestone surface indicative of a cluster of minute vesicles. A skin biopsy shows characteristic changes.

Laboratory diagnosis

The laboratory methods for identification are the same as for herpes simplex; however, the relative utility of the procedures differs for the two viruses:
- Immunofluorescent antibody stains of vesicular fluid,
- VZV IgG and IgM antibody titers,
- Polymerase chain reaction,
- Culture of vesicle fluid,
- Skin biopsy, and
- Tzanck smears

Disseminated Herpes Zoster

Approximately 50% of patients with uncomplicated herpes zoster will have a viremia, with the appearance of 20 to 30 vesicles scattered over the skin surface outside the affected dermatome (Figs 58-59). Patients with Hodgkin's disease are uniquely susceptible to herpes zoster. Furthermore, 15% to 50% of herpes zoster patients with active Hodgkin's disease have disseminated disease involving the skin, lungs, and brain; 10% to 25% of these patients will die if not treated.[39] In patients with other types of cancer, death from herpes zoster is unusual. Patients with cutaneous dissemination have a 5% to 10% risk of pneumonitis (Fig 60), meningitis, hepatitis, and other serious complications.

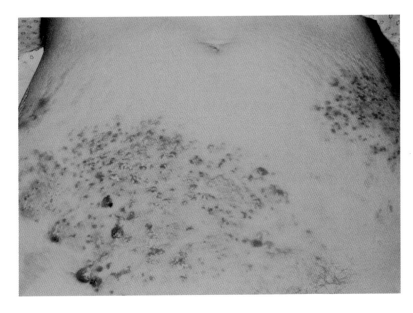

Fig 58.—Disseminated varicella-zoster virus. Grouped and isolated vesicles cover wide areas of the trunk in a random and nondermatomal distribution.

A. Infection in a 23-year-old man with periarteritis nodosa requiring immunosuppressant therapy.

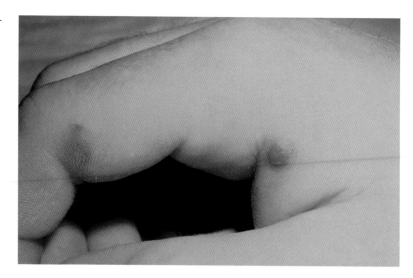

B. Infection in a 47-year-old patient with HIV infection and respiratory failure.

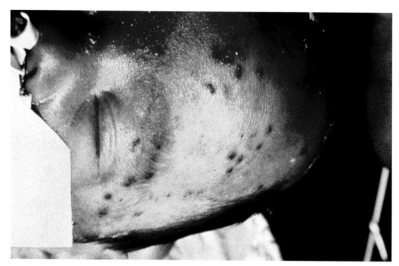

C. Severe infection in a 73-year-old woman with diffuse poorly differentiated lymphocytic lymphoma.

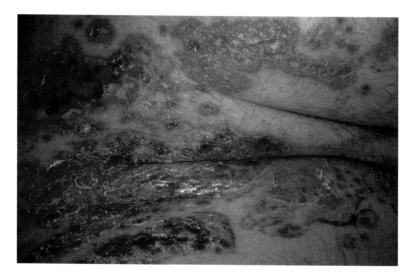

Fig 59.—Disseminated herpes zoster in immunocompromised patients.

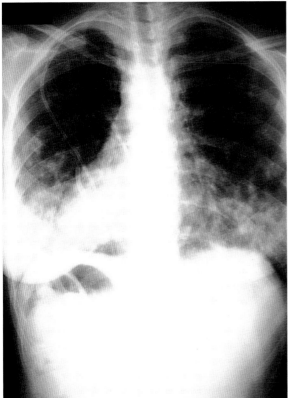

A. Disseminated infection in a 34-year-old patient with breast cancer who was 6 months post bone marrow transplant.

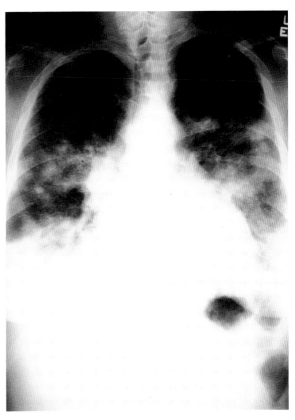

B. Disseminated infection in a 64-year-old patient with acute lymphocytic leukemia who was receiving consolidation chemotherapy.

Fig 60.—Herpes zoster pneumonia in immunocompromised patients.

AIDS and Herpesvirus Infections
Herpes Simplex

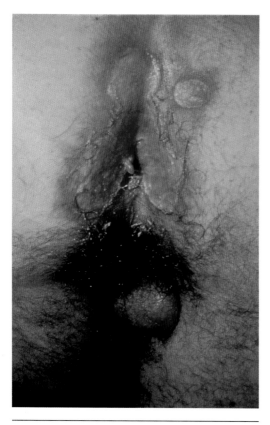

Fig 61.—AIDS and herpes simplex. A broad superficial erosion on opposing surfaces of the anal area. (Courtesy of Benjamin K. Fisher, MD)

Herpes simplex infections are common in patients with AIDS (Figs 61-64). Infection may have an atypical appearance and course, and it can be severe, disfiguring, and persistent. If left untreated, lesions can become deeply erosive and lead to intractable ulcerations. Secondary bacterial infection can further distort the ulcers. Severe progressive perianal and rectal ulcers are seen primarily in homosexual men. Chronic perianal ulcers caused by herpes simplex virus have been erroneously diagnosed as decubitus ulcers. The infection may be widely distributed and be confused with other diseases, such as impetigo.

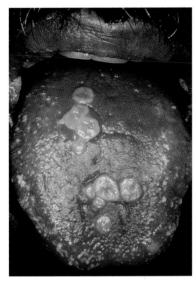

B. Large, deep erosions extend from the nose and the angle of the mouth. (Courtesy of Neal S. Penneys, MD, PhD)

A. Multiple large erosions are present on the surface of the tongue. (Courtesy of Benjamin K. Fisher, MD)

Fig 62.—AIDS and herpes simplex. Chronic, recurrent, mucocutaneous disease.

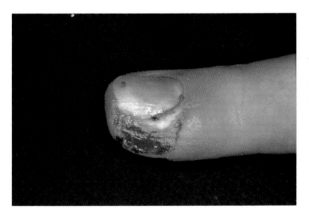

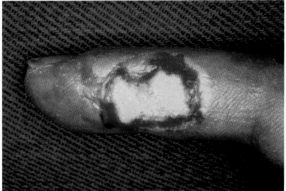

Fig 63.—AIDS and herpes simplex. Superficial and deep chronic herpetic ulcers of the fingers. (Courtesy of Benjamin K. Fisher, MD)

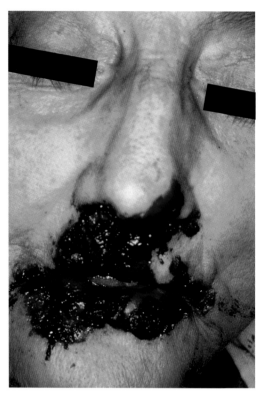

A. Extensive persistent disease.

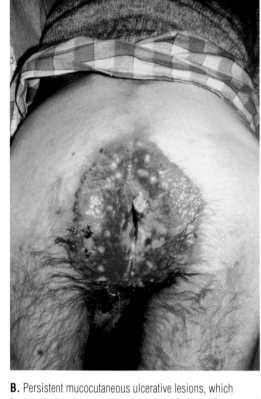

B. Persistent mucocutaneous ulcerative lesions, which frequently develop secondary bacterial infection. (Courtesy of Benjamin K. Fisher, MD)

C. A large chronically infected herpetic ulcer with secondary bacterial infection. (Courtesy of Benjamin K. Fisher, MD)

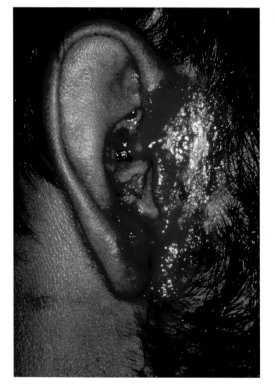

Fig 64.—AIDS and herpes simplex virus infection.

Herpes Zoster

Herpes zoster infection may be an early indicator of HIV disease (Fig 65).[40] It frequently occurs in persons in whom AIDS develops later. The potential for nosocomial transmission with primary varicella and herpes zoster should be kept in mind, particularly in wards where a high proportion of patients are immunocompromised.

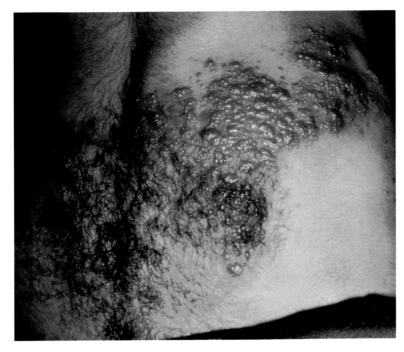

Fig 65.—Herpes zoster infection may be severe, resulting in deep scarring, persistent disseminated lesions, and intractable pain.

Oral Hairy Leukoplakia

Oral hairy leukoplakia is an AIDS-associated lesion. Asymptomatic white, exophytic, and keratinized plaques are situated along the lateral borders of the tongue (Fig 66). More extensive involvement of the oral mucosa can occur. Proliferation of Epstein-Barr virus in the epithelium is thought to be the cause. The lesions may resolve spontaneously. Preliminary studies suggest that intravenous or oral acyclovir is effective treatment, but lesions may recur when treatment is stopped.

Fig 66.—Whitish, nonremovable, verrucous, hairy plaques occur on the sides of the tongue and may resemble a yeast infection.

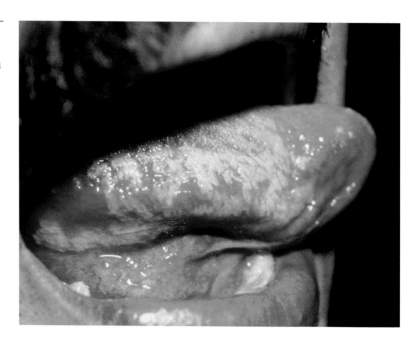

Epstein-Barr Virus Infection

pstein-Barr virus (EBV) is a herpesvirus. EBV infection occurs in more than 90% of the population, and most infections are resolved without any signs or symptoms. Infectious mononucleosis (IM) is the disease most often associated with EBV infection.

Infectious mononucleosis

IM is an acute, self-limited disease of adolescents and young adults. The infection does not recur in healthy individuals. It is transmitted by saliva ("the kissing disease") and is characterized by the classic triad of fever, pharyngitis, and generalized lymphadenopathy (Fig 67). Mild hepatitis causes transient elevation of liver enzymes. Splenomegaly occurs, and patients must avoid trauma that could rupture this organ. The presence of heterophil antibodies confirms the diagnosis. The virus persists in salivary glands and is shed in saliva for months after the infection. Progressive EBV infection can occur in healthy patients but may indicate a deficiency of cellular immunity.[41] Chronic IM is a rare syndrome that arises in previously healthy people. It has distinct features that differentiate it from the common chronic fatigue syndrome.[42,43]

Epidemiology

Age

IM may occur at any age, but most cases occur during adolescence and early adulthood. Preadolescent children resolve a primary EBV infection with few or no symptoms.

Incidence

The incidence of IM is higher in countries with high standards of hygiene such as the United States and western Europe. The majority of people in developing countries are exposed and infected during childhood. The vast majority of these infections are asymptomatic. Unlike other herpesvirus infections, IM does not recur except in immunocompromised individuals such as transplant patients. Cytomegalovirus, human immunodeficiency virus (HIV), and *Toxoplasma gondii* can also cause a mononucleosis-like illness.

Clinical course

Incubation and prodrome

The incubation period is 3 to 7 weeks. A 3- to 5-day prodrome of headache and fatigue is followed by severe sore throat and high fever.

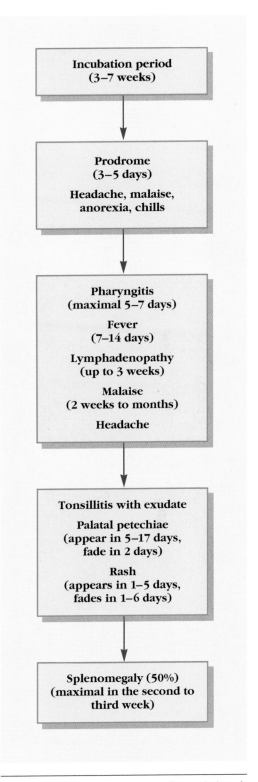

Fig 67.—Infectious mononucleosis. The evolution of signs and symptoms.

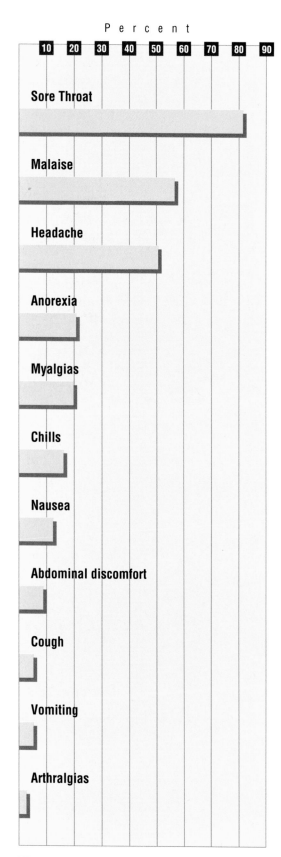

Percent

Fig 68.—Infectious mononucleosis. The most common symptoms.

Active disease

Young children may experience a mild disease with symptoms of an upper respiratory tract infection similar to other common childhood viral infections. The typical presentation of mononucleosis in adolescents consists of fever, sore throat, exudative pharyngotonsillitis, and lymphadenopathy. The pharynx may show diffuse exudate.[44]

Fever. Fever is present in over 70% of patients. It is higher in the afternoon and evening and may reach 102°F to 104°F. A high fever may last for 5 to 10 days, followed by a gradual lysis over 7 to 10 days.

Pharyngitis. The pharyngitis is diffuse. Sore throat with exudative pharyngotonsillitis occurs in the first week of the illness. It is maximal for 5 to 7 days and resolves in 7 to 10 days.

Malaise. Malaise is a striking feature of mononucleosis. Fatigue appears during the prodromal phase and typically resolves in 3 to 4 weeks. Patients with an acute illness typically have a shorter duration of fatigue, but patients who have a course without severe pharyngitis and high fever may remain exhausted for months.

Lymphadenopathy. Firm, tender cervical lymphadenopathy develops and, in many cases, is followed by generalized lymphadenopathy. Nodes are not painful, but are firm and tender. Lymphadenopathy rarely lasts longer than 3 weeks.

Splenomegaly and hepatomegaly. Splenomegaly occurs in about 50% of patients during the second to third week, and hepatomegaly and hepatic tenderness occur in about 10% of patients. Adenopathy or splenomegaly can persist for weeks, well beyond the period of the acute illness. Patients with splenomegaly should avoid contact sports until the spleen shrinks and becomes protected by the rib cage. Generally this requires 4 to 8 weeks.

Rash. About 10% of patients develop a red, macular, and papular eruption that is usually located on the trunk and arms. It appears during the first few days of the illness and fades in 4 to 6 days. A similar but more extensive pruritic, maculopapular eruption occurs in over 90% of patients who are treated with ampicillin and amoxicillin during active IM. The rash appears 5 to 10 days after starting the drug. This is not a long-standing hypersensitivity reaction, and these drugs may be used in the same individual once the viral infection has subsided.

Oral lesions. Petechiae appear on the palate in up to 10% of patients. They appear in 5 to 17 days and rapidly fade in 2 to 4 days.

Other symptoms and signs. The incidence of the many other symptoms and signs is illustrated in Figures 68 and 69.[43] Chronic IM is very rare and not related to the chronic fatigue syndrome.

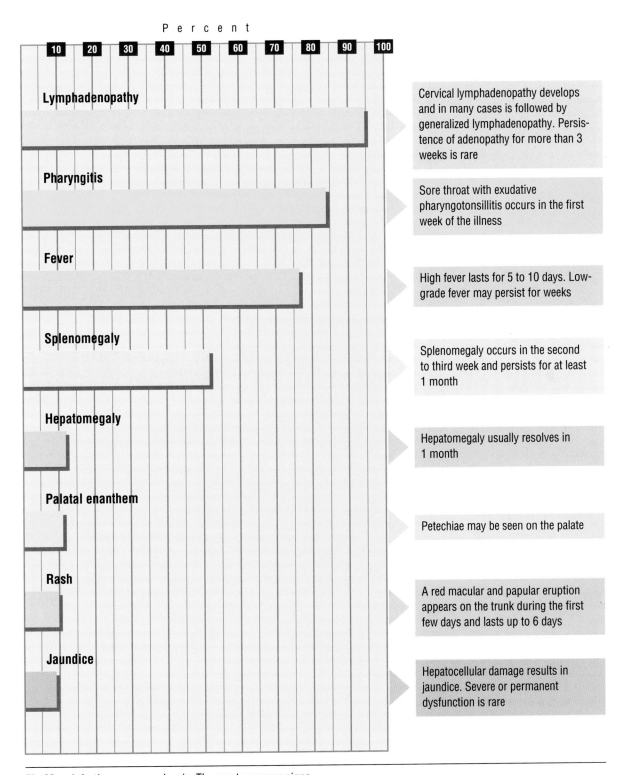

Fig 69.—Infectious mononucleosis. The most common signs.

Complications

Complications of IM (Table 2) are uncommon, but they may be the predominant manifestation of the disease.[45] These complications can arise in healthy patients, but may indicate a deficiency of cellular immunity.

Table 2.— Complications of Infectious Mononucleosis

Cardiac
Myocarditis
Pericarditis

Dermatologic
Acrocyanosis
Ampicillin-associated rash
Cold-mediated urticaria
Leukocytoclastic vasculitis
Leukoplakia
Oral hairy leukoplakia

Hematologic
Aplastic anemia
Autoimmune hemolytic anemia
Granulocytopenia
Hemophagocytic syndrome
Thrombocytopenia

Hepatic
Hepatitis

Immunologic
Anergy
Burkitt's and non-Hodgkin's B- and T-cell lymphomas
Hypergammaglobulinemia
Hypogammaglobulinemia
X-linked and non–X-linked lymphoproliferative syndromes

Neurologic
Cranial nerve palsies, especially Bell's palsy
Encephalitis
Guillain-Barré syndrome
Meningoencephalitis
Mononeuritis multiplex
Optic neuritis
Psychosis
Seizures
Transverse myelitis

Pulmonary
Hilar lymphadenopathy
Laryngotonsillar obstruction
Lymphocytic interstitial pneumonitis
Nasopharyngeal carcinoma
Pleuritis
Pneumonia
Streptococcal pharyngitis

Renal
Glomerulonephritis
Hepatitis
Interstitial nephritis
Massive hepatic necrosis
Reye's syndrome

Splenic
Rupture

Adapted from Straus SE. *Ann Rev Med.* 1992;43:437-449.

Lymphoproliferative disorders

There are several EBV–associated lymphoproliferative diseases, most of which are seen in persons with cellular immune deficiency.[46] EBV–associated B-cell tumors occur in both transplant recipients and AIDS patients. Death results from tumor expansion, immunodeficiency, or infection. Remissions of tumors have been reported with the use of alpha interferon and intravenous gamma globulin.

X-linked lymphoproliferative disease

The X-linked lymphoproliferative syndrome is a rare disease of young boys who develop fulminant mononucleosis.[47] There is B- and T-cell infiltration of organs, and bone marrow displacement. Most patients die of hemorrhage or infection within weeks. Those who survive, die by age 40 of infection, aplastic anemia, hypo- or hypergammaglobulinemia, or lymphomas.

Lymphomas and cancer

Burkitt's lymphoma, non-Hodgkin's B-cell and central nervous system lymphomas, nasopharyngeal carcinoma, and some thymomas have been associated with EBV infection.

Laboratory diagnosis

Atypical lymphocytes and heterophil antibodies

The laboratory diagnosis of acute EBV infectious mononucleosis is based on:

1. An absolute lymphocytosis in which more than 10% of cells are atypical.
2. Heterophil antibody titers of at least 1:56 by the Paul-Bunnell test or positive rapid slide assays such as the Mono-Latex test. These become positive after 1 or 2 weeks.

EBV–specific antibodies

Anti-VCA. Preadolescents or those with neurologic complications or clinically atypical disease may be heterophil negative or lack atypical lymphocytes. EBV–specific antibody studies must be obtained to make an accurate diagnosis. IgM antibodies to the EBV viral capsid antigen (anti-VCA) are diagnostic of a primary EBV infection. They appear early, persist for weeks to months, and do not reappear. Analysis of acute and convalescent sera shows a rise, fall, and a life-long persistence of IgG anti-VCA in titers ranging from 1:10 to 1:2560.[41]

Cytomegalovirus Infection

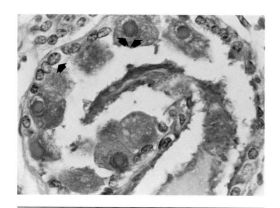

Fig 70.—Cytomegalovirus histology. This kidney section shows normal tubule cells (arrow) and adjacent infected cells with large nuclei that contain the huge (cytomegalic), purplish intranuclear inclusions containing the virus particles (double arrow). (Courtesy of Boris Gueft, MD)

ytomegalovirus (CMV) is a member of the herpesvirus family of viruses. Once acquired during a primary infection, CMV persists indefinitely in host tissues. The sites of latent infection are unknown, but probably involve multiple organs. CMV infections are common, and most are clinically inapparent. CMV can induce asymptomatic and subclinical infections, a mononucleosis-like syndrome, severe birth defects, and disseminated disease in the immunocompromised. Virus replication produces large intranuclear inclusions and smaller cytoplasmic inclusions. The infected cells are enlarged, hence the name cytomegalovirus (Fig 70).

Epidemiology

The virus requires intimate exposure for transmission. Approximately 1% of newborns are infected. Childhood infections are common. Most of the population is infected by puberty.[48] Venereal spread is responsible for most adult infections. Virus may be present in milk, saliva, feces, urine, semen, or cervical secretions.[49] As with other herpesviruses, once infected, an individual probably carries the virus for life. CMV syndromes develop in patients with compromise of T-lymphocyte–mediated immunity. Patients with transplanted organs, lymphoid neoplasms, and acquired immunodeficiencies are at greatest risk.[50]

Congenital CMV infection

Cytomegalic inclusion disease is the most common congenital viral infection. It is seen almost exclusively in infants born to mothers who develop primary infections during pregnancy. Intrauterine fetal infections range from inapparent to severe. Most congenital CMV infections are clinically inapparent at birth. Up to 15% of asymptomatically infected infants develop significant psychomotor, hearing, ocular, or dental abnormalities over the next several years.[49] Less than 10% of infected infants have clinical disease in the neonatal period or at birth. The physical and laboratory findings due to CMV infection of the neonate are similar to other congenital infections. These have been labeled the TORCH syndrome (for *t*oxoplasmosis, *o*ther infections such as syphilis or bacterial sepsis, *r*ubella, *c*ytomegalovirus, and *h*erpes simplex).

Infants with these infections may have hepatosplenomegaly, microcephaly, deafness, chorioretinitis, pneumonitis, hyperbilirubinemia, jaundice, thrombocytopenia, petechiae, and "blueberry muffin" lesions. "Blueberry muffin" lesions are blue-red papules and nodules that last 4 to 6 weeks. They represent dermal erythropoiesis, a process possibly initiated by infection or anemia.

Severely infected infants have mortality rates approaching 30%. Hydrocephalus and intracranial calcifications are poor prognostic indicators. Most survivors have intellectual or hearing difficulties in later years.

CMV mononucleosis

A heterophil-antibody–negative mononucleosis-like syndrome is the most common clinical manifestation of CMV infection in normal hosts beyond the neonatal period. The incubation period is 20 to 60 days, and the illness lasts from 2 to 6 weeks. The disease occurs at all ages, but is most commonly seen in sexually active young adults. There are prolonged high fevers, profound fatigue, malaise, abnormal liver function tests, and atypical lymphocytosis. Myalgias, headache, and splenomegaly also occur, but exudative pharyngitis and cervical lymphadenopathy are less severe than in infectious mononucleosis caused by Epstein-Barr virus. Occasionally a rubelliform rash occurs. Like EBV mononucleosis, CMV mononucleosis patients have a diffuse maculopapular eruption when treated with ampicillin.

CMV infection in the immunocompromised

CMV infection in the immunocompromised is capable of producing a wide spectrum of disease. It may be the most frequent viral pathogen in organ transplantation and is an important pathogen in AIDS patients. Infection may be asymptomatic, produce a mononucleosis-like illness, or involve one or several organs or systems such as the lung, liver, heart, gastrointestinal tract, retina, brain, endocrine system, and skin. The risk of infection is greatest between 1 and 4 months after transplantation. Morbidity is highest in bone marrow transplant recipients and lowest in kidney transplantation. Disease severity is related to the type of immunosuppressive agent and the degree of T-cell suppression. Patients receiving cyclosporin A are less likely to have severe infections than those treated with antithymocyte globulin, a potent suppressor of T lymphocytes. CMV infection has a nonspecific immunosuppressive effect and predisposes patients to serious bacterial and fungal infections. Systemic infections

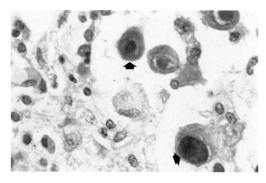

A. Pulmonary alveolus with normal alveolar lining cells and CMV-infected large cells with distinct huge intranuclear viral inclusions (arrows). (Courtesy of Boris Gueft, MD)

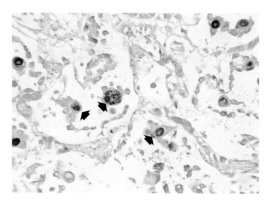

B. Virus is demonstrated by a DNA probe specific for the CMV virus (arrows). The probe is visualized by a brown peroxidase reaction. (Courtesy of Boris Gueft, MD)

Fig 71.—Cytomegalic pneumonia.

begin with fatigue, malaise, night sweats, arthralgias, and fever. Laboratory abnormalities include leukopenia, thrombocytopenia, atypical lymphocytosis, and abnormal liver function tests.

Lung

The lung is the most common organ involved in CMV infection in the immunocompromised patient. Fever, nonproductive cough, dyspnea, and hypoxia herald the onset of lung involvement. The disease may be asymptomatic or rapidly fatal.[51] It is fatal in up to 90% of untreated patients. Concomitance with *Pneumocystis,* especially in the AIDS patient, may occur. A bilateral interstitial pattern is most commonly seen on chest x-ray films. Lung biopsy is required for diagnosis since other opportunistic pathogens can also cause interstitial pneumonia and antibody titers may be low (Fig 71).

Gastrointestinal tract

Gastrointestinal CMV involvement may be localized or extensive, and may involve the esophagus, stomach, intestine, colon, and gallbladder.[52] Nausea, vomiting, and a burning sensation are characteristic of esophagitis. Abdominal cramping, fever, and diarrhea that may be bloody occur with infection of the colon. Ulcers with hemorrhages and perforation can occur anywhere from the esophagus to the rectum. AIDS patients may develop explosive, watery diarrhea. Endoscopy reveals plaque-like pseudomembranes, multiple erosions, and serpiginous ulcers (Fig 72). CMV may be isolated from biopsy material or identified by inclusion bodies in the submucosal endothelium.

Eye

CMV retinitis is an important cause of blindness in immunocompromised patients, especially in AIDS patients and organ transplant recipients. A slowly progressive involvement of the neural retina is usually irreversible and may result in blindness. Examination shows small, opaque, fluffy white areas of granular retinal necrosis or diffuse hemophagic retinitis. CMV must be distinguished from other causes of retinopathy including toxoplasmosis, candidiasis, and herpes simplex virus infection. The diagnosis is based on clinical findings and positive cultures at other sites.[53]

Liver

Hepatitis due to CMV is common in immunocompromised hosts, and many cases are clinically mild and without sequelae. Liver enzyme elevation, hepatomegaly, malaise, vomiting, and lymphocytosis without jaundice or hyperbilirubinemia are seen in these cases. Severe hepatitis and fulminant hepatic failure may occur after liver transplantation.[54] Severe disease is more common after primary infection and in patients who are seronegative and have received a liver graft from a seropositive donor. These patients have positive blood, urine, sputum, or feces cultures. A liver biopsy is required for definitive diagnosis. CMV hepatitis must be distinguished from graft rejection. Infection is treated by decreasing immunosuppression; rejection is treated by increasing immunosuppression.

Laboratory diagnosis

The diagnosis of CMV infection requires laboratory confirmation.[55] Viral culture and demonstrating a serologic rise are the common methods. Nucleic acid hybridization and the polymerase chain reaction are newer tests that are becoming more widely available. They measure viral nucleic acids, and are sensitive and accurate. The virus can be cultured from blood, urine, mouth swabs, buffy coat, biopsy specimens, or the suspected site of infection. CMV is found in the cervix and in semen in some normal adults. Viral excretion from urine and saliva may take place for months to years following illness; therefore, virus isolation does not imply acute infection. Detection of CMV viremia is a better predictor of acute infection. CMV is grown on human fibroblast cultures. Centrifugation culture can now confirm the diagnosis in 16 to 48 hours. The diagnosis can also be made by examination of biopsy tissue and bronchoalveolar lavage fluid for large intranuclear inclusion bodies. Viral antigens can be visualized in these tissue specimens by immunofluorescence.

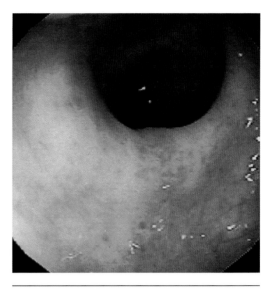

Fig 72.—Cytomegalovirus infection. Endoscopic examination reveals plaque-like pseudomembranes, multiple erosions, and serpiginous ulcers.

Human Herpesvirus Type 6 Infection

Human herpesvirus type 6 (HHV-6) has been established as the cause of roseola infantum. As with other herpesvirus infections, the virus persists after the primary infection. HHV-6 has been isolated from the saliva of more than 85% of asymptomatic immunocompetent adults.[56]

Roseola infantum (infants and children)

Roseola infantum (exanthem subitum, "sudden rash," sixth disease) has been found to be caused by HHV-6. It is the most common exanthematic fever in children under the age of 2. Most cases are asymptomatic or occur without a rash. The disease is sporadic, and the majority of cases occur between the ages of 6 months and 3 years; 75% of babies become infected by 14 months of age.[57] The development of high fever as is seen in roseola is worrisome, but the onset of the characteristic rash is reassuring.

Incubation and prodrome

The incubation period of roseola infantum is 8 days, with a range of 5 to 15 days (Fig 73). There may be mild irritability, but coryza, cough, conjunctivitis, or other symptoms are not present. The prodrome is followed by the sudden onset of high fever of 103°F to 105°F. Most children appear inappropriately well for the degree of temperature elevation, but they may experience slight anorexia or one or two episodes of vomiting. Seizures, probably febrile, sometimes occur. Mild to moderate lymphadenopathy, usually in the occipital regions, begins at the onset of the febrile period and persists until after the eruption has subsided.

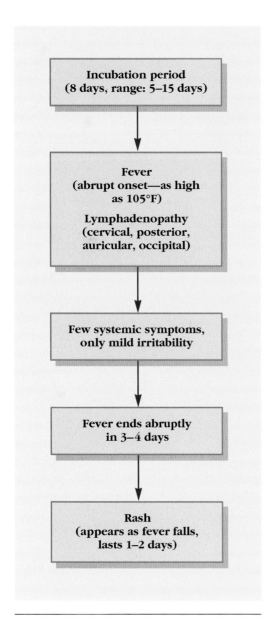

Fig 73.—Exanthem subitum (roseola infantum).

Eruptive phase

The rash begins as the fever subsides. Numerous pale pink, almond-shaped macules appear on the trunk and neck, become confluent, and then fade in a few hours to 2 days without scaling or pigmentation (Figs 74-75). The exanthem may resemble rubella or measles, but the pattern of development, distribution, and associated symptoms of these other exanthematous diseases are different.

HHV-6 mononucleosis

There is serologic evidence that HHV-6 infection in adults and older children is associated with a mononucleosis-like illness.[58] Immunocompetent patients have a spectrum of disease ranging from mild, afebrile illness with nonspecific complaints to 3 months of limited, febrile mononucleosis syndrome. Many have findings of hepatitis and most have atypical lymphocytosis. While most of the manifestations of HHV-6 are mild and self-limited, it is possible that life-threatening disease may occur, particularly in the immunocompromised.

Laboratory diagnosis

Leukocytosis develops at the onset of fever, but leukopenia with a relative lymphocytosis appears as the fever increases and persists until the eruption fades. There is a seroconversion with a primary HHV-6 infection. Virus isolation is a specialized procedure and is not generally available.

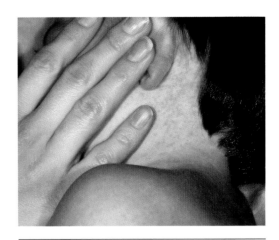

Fig 74.—Roseola infantum. Pale pink macules may appear first on the neck.

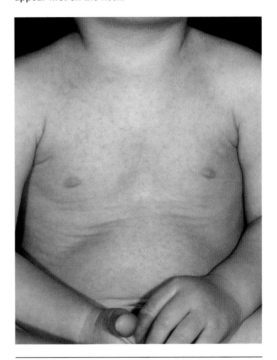

Fig 75.—Roseola infantum. Numerous pale pink,

References

1. Lafferty WE, Coombs RW, Benedetti J, Critchlow C, Corey L. Recurrences after oral and genital herpes simplex virus infection. *N Engl J Med*. 1987; 316(23):1444-1449.

2. Nahasss GT, Goldstein BA, et al. Comparison of Tzanck smear, viral culture, and DNA diagnostic methods in detection of herpes simplex and varicella-zoster infection. *JAMA*. 1992;268:2541-2544.

3. Miura S, Smith CC, et al. Detection of viral DNA within skin of healed recurrent herpes simplex virus infection and erythema multiforme lesions. *J Invest Dermatol*. 1992;98:68-72.

4. Novelli VM, Atherton DJ, Marshall WC. Eczema herpeticum. *Clin Ped*. 1988;27(5):231-233.

5. Sanderson IR, Brueton LA, Savage MO, Harper JI. Eczema herpeticum: a potentially fatal disease. *Br Med J*. 1987;294:693-694.

6. Kagan RJ, Naraqi S, Matsuda T, Jonasson OM. Herpes simplex virus and cytomegalovirus infections in burned patients. *J Trauma*. 1985;Jan 25(1):40-45.

7. Corey L. First-episode, recurrent, and asymptomatic herpes simplex infections. *J Acad Dermatol*. 1988;18:169-172.

8. Prober CG, Sullender WM, Yasukawa LL, Au DS, Yeager AS, Arvin AM. Low risk of herpes simplex virus infections in neonates exposed to the virus at the time of vaginal delivery to mothers with recurrent genital herpes simplex virus infections. *N Engl J Med*. 1987;316(5):240-244.

9. Kulhanjian JA, Soroush V, Au DS, et al. Identification of women at unsuspected risk of primary infection with herpes simplex virus type 2 during pregnancy. *N Engl J Med*. 1992;326(14):916-920.

10. Brown ZA, Benedetti J, Ashley R, et al. Neonatal herpes simplex virus infection in relation to asymptomatic maternal infection at the time of labor. *N Engl J Med*. 1991;324(18):1247-1252.

11. Brown ZA, Vontver LA, Benedetti J, et al. Effects on infants of a first episode of genital herpes during pregnancy. *N Engl J Med*. 1987;317(20):1246-1251.

12. Toltzis P. Current issues in neonatal herpes simplex virus infection. *Clin Perinatology*. 1991;18(2):193-208.

13. Koskiniemi M, Happonen J, Järvenpää A, Pettay O, Vaheri A. Neonatal herpes simplex virus infection: a report of 43 patients. *Pediatr Infect Dis J*. 1989;8(1):30-35.

14. Whitley R, Arvin A, Prober C, et al. Predictors of morbidity and mortality in neonates with herpes simplex virus infections. *N Engl J Med*. 1991; 324(7):450-454.

15. Whitley RJ. Herpes simplex virus infections of the central nervous system. *Drugs*. 1991;42(3):406-427.

16. Sköldenberg B. Herpes simplex encephalitis. *Scand J Infect*. 1991;Suppl 78:40-46.

17. Kimura H, Aso K, Kuzushima K, Hanada N, Shibata M, Morishima T. Relapse of herpes simplex encephalitis in children. *Pediatrics*. 1992;89(5): 891-894.

18. Anderson NE, Powell KF, et al. A polymerase chain reaction assay of cerebrospinal fluid in patients with suspected herpes simplex encephalitis. *J Neurol Neurosurg Psychiatry*. 1993;56:520-525.

19. Puchhammer-Stockl E, Heinz FX, et al. Evaluation of the polymerase chain reaction for diagnosis of herpes simplex virus encephalitis. *J Clin Microbiol*. 1993;31:146-148.

20. Aslanzadeh J, Osmon DR, et al. A prospective study of the polymerase chain reaction for detection of herpes simplex virus in cerebrospinal fluid submitted to the clinical virology laboratory. *Mol Cell Probes*. 1992;6:367-373.

21. McBane RD, Gross JB. Herpes esophagitis: clinical syndrome, endoscopic appearance, and diagnosis in 23 patients. *Gastrointestinal Endoscopy*. 1991;37:600-603.

22. Galbraith JCT, Shafran SD. Herpes simplex esophagitis in the immunocompetent patient: report of four cases and review. *Clin Inf Dis*. 1992;14:894-901.

23. Chase RA, Pottage JC, Haber MH, Kistler G, Jensen D, Levin S. Herpes simplex viral hepatitis in adults: two case reports and review of the literature. *Rev Infect Dis*. 1987;9(2):329-333.

24. Johnson JR, Egaas S, Gleaves CA, Hackman R, Bowden RA. Hepatitis due to herpes simplex virus in marrow-transplant recipients. *Clin Infec Dis*. 1992;14:38-45.

25. Kusne S, Schwartz M, Breinig MK, et al. Herpes simplex virus hepatitis after solid organ transplantation in adults. *J Infec Dis*. 1991;163:1001-1007.

26. Jacques SM, Qureshi F. Herpes simplex virus hepatitis in pregnancy: a clinicopathologic study of three cases. *Human Pathology*. 1992;23(2):183-187.

27. Corey L. Herpes simplex viruses. In: Braunwald E, et al, eds. *Harrison's Principles of Internal Medicine*. 11th ed. New York, New York: McGraw Hill; 1987.

28. Croen KD, Straus SE. Varicella-zoster virus latency. *Annu Rev Microbiol*. 1991;45:265-282.

29. Feldman S, Hughes WT, Daniel CB. Varicella in children with cancer: seventy-seven cases. *Pediatrics*. 1975;56:388-397.

30. Stagno S, Whitley RJ. Herpes virus infections of pregnancy. Part II: herpes simplex virus and varicella-zoster virus infections. *N Engl J Med*. 1985;313(21):1327-1330.

31. Rothe MJ, Feder HM, Grant-Kels JM. Oral acyclovir therapy for varicella and zoster infections in pediatric and pregnant patients: a brief review. *Ped Derm*. 1991;8(3):236-242.

32. Puchhammer-Stockl E, Popow-Kraupp T, et al. Detection of varicella-zoster virus DNA by polymerase chain reaction in the cerebrospinal fluid of patients suffering from neurological complications associated with chicken pox or herpes zoster. *J Clin Microbiol*. 1991;29:1513-1516.

33. Shoji H, Honda Y, et al. Detection of varicella-zoster virus DNA by polymerase chain reaction in the cerebrospinal fluid of patients with herpes zoster meningitis. *J Neurol.* 1992;239:69-70.

34. Sawyer MH, Wu YN, et al. Detection of varicella-zoster virus DNA in the oropharynx and blood of patients with varicella. *J Infect Dis.* 1992;166:885-888.

35. Ragozzino MW, Melton LJ, Kurland LT, Chu CP, Perry HO. Risk of cancer after herpes zoster. *N Engl J Med.* 1982;307(7):393-397.

36. Rusthoven JJ, Ahlgren P, Elhakim T, et al. Varicella-zoster infection in adult cancer patients. *Arch Intern Med.* 1988;148:1561-1566.

37. Weller TH. Varicella and herpes zoster. *N Engl J Med.* 1983;309(23):1434-1440.

38. Galer BS, Portenoy RK. Acute herpetic and postherpetic neuralgia: clinical features and management. *Mount Sinai J Med.* 1991;58(3):257-266.

39. Mazur MH, Dolin R. Herpes zoster at the NIH: a 20-year experience. *Am J Med.* 1978;65:738-744.

40. Melby M, et al. Risk of AIDS after herpes zoster. *Lancet.* 1987;1:728-731.

41. Okano M, Thiele GM, Davis JR, Grierson HL, Purtillo DT. Epstein-Barr virus and human diseases: recent advances in diagnosis. *Clin Microbiol Rev.* 1988;1:300-312.

42. Schooley RT, Carey RW, Miller G, et al. Chronic Epstein-Barr virus infections associated with fever and interstitial pneumonitis. *Ann Intern Med.* 1986;104:636-643.

43. Straus SE. The chronic mononucleosis syndrome. *J Infect Dis.* 1988;157:405-412.

44. Schooley RT, Dolin R. Epstein-Barr virus (infectious mononucleosis). In: Mandell GL, Douglas RG Jr, Bennett JE, eds. *Principles and Practice of Infectious Diseases.* 3rd ed. New York, NY: Churchill Livingstone; 1990:1182-1185.

45. Straus SE. Acute progressive Epstein-Barr virus infections. *Ann Rev Med.* 1992;43:437-449.

46. Cohen JI. Epstein-Barr virus lymphoproliferative disease associated with acquired immunodeficiency. *Medicine.* 1991;70:137-160.

47. Purtilo DT, DeFlorio D Jr, Huff LM, et al. Variable phenotypic expression of an X-linked lymphoproliferative syndrome. *N Engl J Med.* 1977;297:1077-1081.

48. Stagno S. Cytomegalovirus infection: a pediatrician's perspective. *Curr Probl Pediatr.* 1986;16:629-637.

49. Zaia JA. Epidemology and pathogenesis of cytomegalovirus disease. *Semin Hematol.* 1990;27(suppl1):5-10.

50. Sissons JGP, Borysiewcz LK. Human cytomegalovirus infection. *Thorax.* 1989;44:241-246.

51. Weiner RS, Bortin MM, Gale RP, et al. Interstitial pneumonitis after bone marrow transplantation. Assessment of risk factors. *Ann Intern Med.* 1986;104:168-175.

52. Kaplan CS, Petersen EA, Icenogle TB, et al. Gastrointestinal cytomegalovirus infection in the heart and heart-lung transplant recipients. *Arch Intern Med.* 1989;149:2095-2100.

53. Bloom JN, Palestine AG. The diagnosis of cytomegalovirus retinitis. *Ann Intern Med.* 1988;109:963-969.

54. Stratta RJ, Shaeter MS, Markin RS, et al. Clinical patterns of cytomegalovirus disease after liver transplantation. *Arch Surg.* 1989;125:1443-1450.

55. Drew WL. Diagnosis of cytomegalovirus infection. *Rev Infect Dis.* 1988;10(suppl 3):S468-475.

56. Levy JA, Ferro F, Greenspan D, et al. Frequent isolation of HHV-6 from saliva and high seroprevalence of the virus in the population. *Lancet.* 1990;ii:1047-1050.

57. Okuno T, Takahashi K, Balachandra K, et al. Seroepidemology of human herpesvirus 6 infection in normal children and adults. *J Clin Microbiol.* 1989;27:651-653.

58. Niederaman JC, Liu C-R, Kaplan MH, et al. Clinical and serological features of human herpesvirus 6 infection in three adults. *Lancet.* 1988;ii:817-819.